COCKTAILS & DREAMS

COCKTAILS
YANGDUP LAMA & GITANJALI CHATURVEDI
& DREAMS
The Ultimate
Indian Cocktail Book
wisdom
tree

First published 2014

ISBN 978-81-8328-350-2

Published by
Wisdom Tree
4779/23, Ansari Road
Darya Ganj, New Delhi-110 002
Ph.: 23247966/67/68
wisdomtreebooks@gmail.com

Printed in India

Contents

Foreword *vii*

Introduction *viii*

Liquor and Lipstick 1

Raising the Bar 3

Getting Set ~ Bars & Beyond 5

Know Your Poison 23

Cocktails & Dreams 37

Glossary *147*

Acknowledgements *148*

Foreword

Cocktails are on everyone's lips, so to speak, in the second decade of the twenty-first century. They are trendy, hip, in vogue and there's no better sign that you're a success in life than being known to the bartenders in a good cocktail bar. Cocktails, and people's love for them, is where it's at.

This phenomenon, though, is a very recent thing. Even in London and New York, the cocktail revolution didn't really get off the ground until less than a decade ago. And in India, the cocktail trend is even newer than that. How does something like this get traction, you might wonder. How come one day we're all happy sipping a gin and tonic or perhaps a nice old-fashioned whiskey cocktail and the next day our bartenders are handing us menus filled with drinks calling for tea-infused Tequila that are topped off with an asparagus foam?

I'll tell you how these things start: They start slowly and they start with passion. They start with people such as Yangdup Lama ~ a friend and kindred spirit. Yangdup has made his mark on the global cocktail culture and he continues to push the envelope in India, bringing new ideas to the party and encouraging other bartenders to bring more passion into their craft. Passion is what drives him, and it's what drives this fabulous business of being of service to our guests.

I'm thrilled that Yangdup teamed up with Gitanjali Chaturvedi to bring us this book. It will serve to detail the role of Indian bartenders to the global bartending community and, years from now, people in the service industry will no doubt be poring over its pages to see how the cocktail revolution took off in India.

When you use this book to make drinks for yourself and your loved ones, please remember what the authors advise: If you make the drink with love in your heart, your guest will literally taste that love in the drink. There's a good reason that you think your grandmother was the best cook in the world, you know, and it has nothing to do with her culinary skills.

I'll hand you over to Yangdup and Gitanjali now and they'll show you how to make great cocktails and dream fabulous dreams.

With lotsa love from gaz regan.

Gary Regan

Introduction

The tradition of drinking ~ preparing, consuming and offering alcohol to guests and deities ~ in India, is an ancient one. There is still a strong culture of fermenting cereals such as rice, barley and millet among tribal communities in central and northeast India, and of tapping toddy palm and extracting the nectar of the mahua flower for fermentation. Protector spirits are offered alcohol among hill communities, particularly in Nepal and Tibet. Among Hindus, Lord Bhairava is supposedly partial to country liquor. It keeps him appeased. However, these local brews ~ raksi, chhang, mahua ~ are not commercial. They are prepared at home, have a short shelf life and are neither stored nor bottled. And because every home has its own recipe for brewing, there is no consistency in taste or alcohol content. There are exceptions. Feni, a spirit made from the juice of the cashew apple, is bottled and sold commercially, but its sale is restricted only to the state of Goa as it is considered 'country liquor'. The Sri Lankan coconut arrack has done better. With a taste that is considered to be a blend between rum and whisky, it is set to conquer the markets of the UK and the USA.

In mainland India, however, consuming alcohol socially is a fairly recent phenomenon. Fifteen years ago, if a middle class Indian family was looking for a groom for their daughter ~ usually fair-complexioned and convent educated ~ chances were that they would be looking for a well-settled (read, government job) teetotaller and non-smoker. A government job ensured you never earned enough to be lured by the 'vice' of drinking or smoking and would probably hand over your entire salary to your wife at the beginning of each month. To enjoy an occasional drink back then meant, you were a depressed alcoholic, who chose liquor as an escape mechanism.

Popular culture only reinforced this belief; generations of Hindi cinema portrayed drinking in a stereotypical way. How many of us recall an angry Bollywood hero drinking to get over heartbreak? Or foolishly challenging a villain to a fight and getting thrashed in the process? Only the suave Amitabh Bachchan could charm Parveen Babi with a nonsensical song in *Amar, Akbar, Anthony*. But he was perhaps the only exception. The beautiful Meena Kumari cut a rather tragic figure as she took to drinking to soothe herself from the pain of a perverse husband in *Sahib, Biwi aur Ghulam*. And then there were drunken comics ~ Keshto Mukherjee and Johnny Walker, who stumbled about, blabbered and made a ridiculous spectacle of themselves. *Hum Log*, an iconic drama aired in the early 1980s, had an inebriated character who was not only despotic but also utterly dysfunctional. *Nukkad*, another popular TV soap opera from that time, featured Khopri, a character who is never sober. Naturally, he is filthy, inarticulate and never taken seriously. The message was clear: Drinking is bad. If you drink, you have a bad family life, an awful professional life and nobody is attracted to you. If you drink, you're a loser.

Things are different today. We have witnessed this interesting turn of events. Growing up, our friends would sneak alcohol, usually rum, out of their fathers' bars that we would mix with coke or water and consume surreptitiously in locations that should not be revealed. Some of us, who were slightly bolder and certain that nobody would report us to adults, visited Olympia on Park Street (Calcutta) for a beer or two. Some of us had kind uncles and aunts who indulged us on occasion: 'You're eighteen, have a glass of wine!' Music to the ears! Being thus invited meant you were really an adult. It was this elite club that we all wished to belong to and drinking was just one way of feeling we had come of age. Getting drunk and acting in a silly manner was always unhip and unsexy. We pitied people who didn't know their limit and ended up with their heads inside the toilet after a drink too many. Even so, most of us have been down that route! Drinking and driving was taboo. We did see a few of our acquaintances crashing cars and bikes and having their bodies rearranged.

We were growing up as India was opening up slowly, but very surely, to embrace the modern and new. Foreign brands were launching their products in the country in the 1990s.

As Bacardi breezed into our lives, giving us an option other than the dark but venerable Old Monk, we experienced for the first time ~ the Mojito. Somewhere in the Western Ghats and in the ample lap of the Deccan, grape was being cultivated for wine. Clearly, the Indian consumer was ready for heady experiences with alcohol. In the last five years, with India's phenomenal economic growth, luxury brands have started to explore markets in the country among the discerning youth that enjoys single malts, vodka and hand-crafted beer.

No longer considered evil or the last resort of the pathetic, addictive loser, alcohol is now a means to socialise, entertain and even experiment. So, it isn't unusual that fine dining restaurants will endeavour to match their menu with appropriate alcohol. Cocktail bars have opened in metropolitan cities, offering choices that go beyond the whisky-soda or rum-coke. Martinis ~ stirred not shaken, Cosmopolitans and Margaritas are mixed as often as Piña Coladas, Side Cars, Sea Breezes, Whisky Sours and Black Russians. And it is common to see women enjoy a drink as much as men. Nightclubs often entice women with free drinks on a few evenings. 'Happy Hour' ~ when you get a deal on drinks ~ has also successfully crept into the bar lingo in India. Walk into a bar at 6 pm and you will find office-goers dropping in for drinks and conversation. The drone of chatter and laughter is only drowned by DJs when the happy hours are over. A drink does lift your spirits.

Fifteen years ago, the food and beverage (F&B) industry was just as conservative as the rest of the country vis-à-vis alcohol. For a long time, India did not have professional bartenders in leading international hotel chains, even though these positions existed abroad. Today, there are designated bartenders in most leading hotels. Even so, this profession still does not attract the best talent. You become a bartender only if you are interested in alcohol or the job gives you some kind of a high. The tips are good. But you have to be prepared to listen to many stories from a variety of people. You must know how to say the right thing at the right time and ensure your client drinks responsibly ~ it's more important that he goes home happy rather than drunk. A real passion for mixing drinks however, is still uncommon. We hope that this will change and that people who really enjoy shaking and pouring a drink will opt to become bartenders.

Indians have clearly displayed a preference for brown spirits with molasses ~ whisky and rum score over brandy and gin. Vodka, however, has made a reasonable dent among urban youth, pushed largely by brands such as Smirnoff, Vladivar, Absolut, Grey Goose, Ciroc and Belvedere. What has gained maximum popularity in the last decade, however, is beer. Popular among the young crowd, it gives you the biggest bang for your buck. You can guzzle beer slower than you sip a cocktail ~ simply because of the quantity in a single pint ~ and still get a buzz. Bengaluru probably led the way in revolutionising the beer and pub culture, but other metropolitan cities soon caught on. Even Patiala, the city that has immortalised the peg, today has a fair share of bars and pubs. As also the temple city of Madurai ~ drinking isn't a taboo as it used to be.

Even though India has changed, the perception towards alcohol in government policy has not adjusted accordingly. Gujarat has always been a dry state; the only place where you can purchase alcohol legally is in a chemist shop. Taxes and duties on alcohol are high and the nation observes a few mandatory 'dry' days. On regular days, there are restrictions on how long a restaurant or club can remain open. A home bar ~ if you do enjoy drinking and entertaining ~ is an easy way out. And you don't run the risk of being breathalysed or fined by the police on your way back! But you do miss out on the fun of watching professional bartenders shake and show off their skills behind the bar in a cool location. Until we achieve that balance of working and playing hard, here are a few tips and recipes to make your evenings enjoyable and memorable.

Please drink responsibly, we always advise our friends to tread the middle path of moderation.

My first alcoholic drink was Old Monk with cola at Calcutta's iconic Saturday Club. The Summer Carnival was on; I was with friends who were also experiencing their first so-called cocktail. I sipped gingerly through a straw. The rum was barely palpable through the highly sweetened cola. Yet, I don't remember enjoying the drink. Everybody else on the other hand, seemed to be quite merry. In hindsight, it was perhaps the thrill of tasting something forbidden that was giving them a high.

Liquor and Lipstick

Gitanjali

A few years later, the feisty Moon Moon Sen invited my sister and me to our first real cocktail party. 'Wear dresses,' she told us. I have vivid memories of accessorising our clothes with jewellery borrowed from our mother. We got to the Dev Varma apartment on Harrington Street where Riya expertly applied the finishing touches to our make-up ~ a skill that I still haven't mastered. At the party, we discovered that all the women had dressed down. 'Nobody wears dresses here,' I observed. 'That's because they don't know,' replied Moon Moon, 'That cocktail parties are all about dressing up.' Again, I remember the deep-fried shrimps better than the alcohol, but I haven't forgotten that fashion is an integral part of the cocktail affair.

Moon Moon was ahead of her times but I am glad she offered us this important grain of wisdom. Today, women have finally begun to dress up for cocktail events in India. They flaunt their dresses, accessories and hairdos ~ the whole shebang.

Many cocktail evenings followed my initiation ~ while in JNU, a few of us decided to organise a little party on Valentine's Day. We girls offered to bartend, JNU was a safe haven where the only risk one ran was to be featured in a pamphlet the following day. Happily, that didn't happen. My friends and I organised the alcohol and studied a few recipes that we could prepare without much fuss. We didn't have peg measures, so we improvised with test tubes pinched from the Life Sciences lab. And we did fix some mean cocktails. Towards the end of the evening, when we ran out of mixes, we served shots. How cool was that? By the time I finished with university, I had acquired the skills to prepare a few good cocktails. I also developed a taste for Gin and Tonic ~ with freshly squeezed lime (see page 74) and the Long Island Tea.

In the course of my travels ~ first as a wide-eyed youngster and now as a woman of the world (I hope) ~ I have raised a glass in the strangest, often surreal situations. In coastal Tuticorin, more famous for its pearls than alcohol, I shared Golconda sherry with a few Catholic priests who strummed one gospel after another. A friend once took me to a rather swish bar in Ashgabat where one had vodka under the watchful eyes of the KGB. Several stories below, the Turkmen capital twinkled back at us in its energy-abundant splendour. In Nuwara Eliya, in up-country Sri Lanka, the bartender used a limited selection of alcohol with an equally small number of mixes ~ coconut water, watermelon juice or pineapple juice. He dressed these cocktails with little paper umbrellas fashioned out of toothpicks. That was all that the bar could offer, apart from cricket. While trekking in lower Mustang, I've had hot buttered rum with a magnificent view of the Annapoorna range. In the Helambu region, also in Nepal, we were invited to share a rather foul raksi with the proprietor of the lodge where we were staying. At a ballet in Moscow, I was forced to drain a rather large shot of vodka with lightning speed during the interval so as to return to my seat on time. How my throat burned!

My long association with the polio eradication initiative led me, on one occasion, to create a cocktail inspired by the oral polio vaccine. Foremost on my mind was getting the magenta colour right and giving the concoction a somewhat sour taste, quite like the OPV. We mixed vodka with fresh lime water/soda sweet and cranberry juice to obtain the magenta hue. Fresh lime water/soda sweet contributed to the slight tanginess, which worked quite well. The drink was shaken and poured into a chilled cocktail glass and served without garnish. We downed it in two large gulps ~ way more than the two drops prescribed for OPV!

Perhaps my most innovative cocktail experiences were in Afghanistan. The alcohol was rationed severely and we had to improvise. We used whatever we found to fix our drinks. So, if we found Campari, we mixed it with orange juice or any other juice. Sometimes we even used Malibu and pineapple juice to ease the taste of a rather bitter (and somewhat soapy) Campari. There was always lots of fresh juice available ~ pomegranate, watermelon, apple, grape ~ we'd use these liberally with just about anything. And fruits made great garnishes. Since we lived in a community, we often made enormous punches where anything would go. We also made a rather sophisticated punch out of Mojito. If you feel creative (and sufficiently inspired) do try the following recipe that we innovated.

The UNOCA Cocktail

Ingredients

Campari	30 ml
Malibu	30 ml
Fresh pineapple juice	90 ml
Soda	To top
Fresh lime wedges	2
Fresh strawberries	3
Mint sprigs	2 sprigs

Method

Cut the strawberries into quarters and drop in a tall glass filled with ice. Press the mint sprigs and drop into the glass followed by a squeeze of fresh lime wedges. Add the Malibu, Campari and pineapple juice and stir well. Top with soda and serve.

You can vary this with fresh orange juice to fix the traditional Campari Orange, add vodka (instead of Malibu) to tone down the bitterness of the Campari. The other ingredients ~ fresh strawberries, lime wedges and mint ~ work just as well in this variation.

More than anything, it is the company that makes the cocktail experience so memorable. It brings out hidden talent ~ or so we think ~ as people transform into rock stars and divas, or the slightly more melancholic amongst us, into poets and philosophers. You do need a good bartender, however. Each one of us, somewhere, has it in us to be a fairly decent mixologist ~ in the right circumstances.

Had I not been a bartender, I would have been a monk. Either way, I would have been a spiritualist! I was introduced to bartending the day I joined the Hyatt Regency, Delhi, in 1996. The Polo Lounge was short of manpower and I was the freshman that had to be inserted somewhere useful. The hottest selling drink at the bar those days was the Caipiroschka. I still remember a bunch of regulars who, with every visit to the bar, would boost our tip box for the whole week! Laval Lim Hon, someone I consider my guru, likened bartending to an art form.

Raising the Bar

Yangdup

There are three facets to this art: The bar, the bartender and the customer. The Polo Lounge did, indeed fulfil all these criteria ~ tastefully designed, it attracted a diverse mix of hotel guests from across the world and local regulars. The resident bartender (called a Bar Captain in those days) worked his magic, swiftly fixing one artistic drink after another.

Pouring drinks for customers did not come too easily. Even more difficult was remembering the clients and their tabs. In the early days, I often forgot to charge my customers for their drinks which led to a major discrepancy of a few spirits, but I was a fast learner and moved quite quickly to the bar counter. My first cocktail was a variation of the Singapore Sling. I built this drink in a tall glass with ice, gin, fresh lime juice, sugar syrup, soda and cherry brandy. Subsequently, at another bar, I saw the bartender shake the drink with juices rather than pouring any carbonated drink. My first lesson, thus, was that a cocktail could have several versions with an unending range of flavours.

The best part of being a bartender is being the centre of the fun and action around the bar counter. The world comes to you, good, bad and ugly ~ businessmen, artists, politicians, sportspeople and entertainers. You get to know all your clients and build relationships with them. I particularly remember my three best customers ~ a Belgian shoe designer, an Indian advocate at the Supreme Court and an American who was working in India with a power company ~ all in their late forties. None of them ordered cocktails. The American always stuck to his beer and the others preferred straight drinks. They never talked shop but instead, had conversations about culture, politics and of course, women. Then there was troublesome Jerry who would gulp down six double gin and tonics but never pay for his last drink. We tried everything from not clearing his glasses to keeping count of the stirrers for each drink. Nothing would work. He would get aggressive if we gave him the correct count and turn into a complete monster. We finally got round to taming him by presenting him with a bill after every drink. He would meekly pay without protest!

The initial years behind the bar counter are about learning from all angles. From cocktail and beverage books, bottles old and new, seniors at the bar and, most importantly, the people who patronise the bar. There were a few who have taught me how to be a good mixologist. Angela was a cocktail freak who taught me how to fix the Michelada and Clamato with seasoning that she brought with her from Mexico. The Fifth Floor Smash was a cocktail taught to me by a crew member of the British Airways who wanted to relive her bartending days at university.

In the summer of 1999, I left the Hyatt to enter the world of freelance bartending. I already had several offers from regulars to manage the bar at their private events. I knew that it was important to get the bar right at functions. The customer too, by then, had understood this and was willing to spend a fair amount of money on a good bar. What I would earn from mobile bartending would be at least four times what the hotel was paying me. It was time to go.

At the same time, India was changing. The party scene was evolving, weddings were getting bigger and event managers and other professionals were managing these grand affairs. Commercially, it seemed right to enter this 'wedding' arena even though it is a completely different ball game with several challenges. Every element of the bar needs to be managed personally ~ the variety of booze, its quality and quantity, the size of the bar and logistics. Since guests are not required to pay for their drinks at private events, orders come in bulk. The biggest challenge for the bartender is to control spillage and spoilage apart from fixing drinks for an average of over 500 guests at most times. We work closely with designers, planners and event managers. It is a stressful job especially when, as a bar expert, one is at times forced to manage the customer as much as a bunch of bartenders at various bars.

What are parties in India like? We Indians tend to go completely overboard if we have money. From luxury brands to limited edition and handcrafted spirits, wines and champagnes, to the lavish spread of food, we know how to splurge on parties. You need to be rather generous to serve large quantities of fine food and wine to large gatherings over a number of days. Indian hosts also want their parties to be talked about, which accounts for such vast expenses that they are willing to incur on a birthday, anniversary or wedding. The alcohol inventory for these parties at times exceeds the store requisition of alcohol of top hotels with successful food and beverage operations. No other place in the world can rival India in hosting large, opulent private events. I've managed a gathering of approximately 3000 people with seven operational bars and about a 100 bartenders and ensured an unending flow of alcohol. That is the scale of parties in India. But such opulence is largely a north Indian phenomenon. In the south, the scale is large but the expenditure on alcohol and the investment in the bar is marginal.

I've often wondered how I can manage busy bars in such grandiose events. How do I suppress the urge to tell a customer that he may be ordering a weird cocktail? I've fixed, for instance, single malt with orange juice for a customer on one occasion. I am constantly amazed at the popularity of whisky served half with soda and half with water. It seems to make no sense. There are countless bizarre requests, but I simply do my job. When most bartenders would perhaps get overwhelmed with the pressures at the bar in India, I've over time, learned to keep my cool. I have also learned from the Indian guests I've served. The recipe for the Desi Bloody Mary (see page 118) is a tribute to my customers who inspired me to improvise the traditional recipe with coriander, rock salt and chaat masala to prepare a fabulous afternoon cocktail. This also works very well with Indian wedding events.

India's love affair with cocktails is just about beginning. The richness of variety in tastes in the country offers a good future for the cocktail revolution. It is exciting to witness this revolution, as this is all about being creative, using one's imagination and dipping into the vast culture and tradition of Indian spices, flavours and essences to fix original, artistic drinks. The next time you pick up the cocktail shaker, think of how you can innovate and make your drink extra special.

Getting Set ~ Bars & Beyond

BOMBAY
SAPPHIRE
Distilled
LONDON
DRY GIN
IMPORTED
Nocino
della Cristina
ACARDI
8
ANGOSTURA
1919
PREMIUM RUM
agatiba
Zacapa
Sauza
HECHO EN MEXICO
FRESH BLUE AGAVE
TEQUILA SILVER
HINE
OBAN

Many years ago, a friend from the Caribbean went to a reputed bar in the Indian capital and ordered a Mojito. He thought, quite naturally, that he would be given the real thing. Imagine his horror when what arrived tasted like fresh lime soda with a profusion of mint, lime and ice! A bar of that class ought to have known how to fix a Mojito. He was indignant. As he went on to provide a tutorial to the bartender, he also pointed out that the bars in the country offer many surprises to customers. One can never accurately predict whether the experience will be altogether satisfying. How can you tell a good bar from a regular rum and

Unless a bar advertises itself as a cocktail bar, we recommend that you do not experiment with your first drink. The decor and ambience can sometimes be misleading as also the elaborate menu cards. Order safe. If the bartender gets a simple order right, whisky on the rocks or a gin and tonic, for instance, chances are he could be tasked with a complicated cocktail. Chat with the bartender and ask him what he'd recommend. He is likely to ask you for your preferred choice of alcohol before he fixes you a cocktail. You are unlikely to go wrong there. If you have a preferred method of preparing your cocktail, share this with the bartender. He is likely to fix your drink right. Check out the alcohol on display before you decide what to order. Observe other customers. If you see complex cocktails arriving at their table, feel free to experiment. But if what you see is a lot of whisky soda or rum coke, play safe. You'd be safer with a Screwdriver. Finally, be realistic. It is very unlikely that a Chinese restaurant will fix mean cocktails. A Spanish or Italian restaurant may stock wine and do a few basic drinks, but if the focus is food, the drink may not be extraordinary.

There is something that must be said for bars and spaces that encourage people to unwind over a drink. A good bar will foster bonhomie among its customers. The music is either subdued or live. You will see people participating and interacting. While it is possible that the drinks served are great, it is the ambience and energy at the bar that attract customers. The bar is likely to be well lit (not brightly lit, but just the right amount of light that allows you to see what you're drinking) and you can actually see the face of the person you have a conversation with. What's better is that you can even hear him. Such bars will never go out of fashion.

More than anything, good bars are gender neutral. Most bars in India have more male customers ~ women often get stares, especially if they are unescorted. While there are spaces where women can comfortably let their hair down, we suggest that your guard must never go down. Because of how they're built physiologically, women tend to absorb alcohol faster than men and consequently get tiddly-pommed easily. Pace your drink and always drink water ~ that will help you stay sober longer. At the risk of sounding preachy ~ if you are a woman anywhere in the world, do observe what the bartender puts in your cocktail, always down your drink before heading to the loo and remember that alcohol has often been blamed for accidents that were not meant to happen.

Bar etiquette

- Know your limit ~ drink to enjoy, not to abuse
- Chat with the bartender, let him know your preferences
- Take your time to order your drink
- Understand how your body responds to different spirits before you mix your drinks
- Don't consume alcohol in a single gulp, savour and enjoy the spirit
- Alcohol consumption requires companions ~ drink with a friend, keep water on the side and be sure to snack along

THE HOME BAR

If you are passionate about your drink and enjoy entertaining friends, we recommend you set up a bar at home. Usually the amount of space determines the size of the bar, but with a little planning and imagination, one can have good-sized home bars to very compact ones with all the basics integrated within a small space. You could choose between an old-fashioned wood finish or a delicate glass bar. What is important is how you stock it up with alcohol and bar tools. Everything beyond this depends on space, budget and interest.

Here are the specifics that go into making a complete bar:

Tools

The Cocktail Shaker

A shaker which comes in various shapes, sizes and styles. The most common cocktail shaker is the three-piece or combination shaker, also called the Old English Cocktail Shaker. A great set to have at home, it is good for mixing a few classic drinks, one at a time. It has a base glass that can take enough liquid for two to three measures of spirits, a middle cap with an inbuilt strainer to hold the ice when doing drinks straight up and a top cap to hold everything inside while shaking the drink.

The Boston Cocktail Shaker

This consists of a big glass and a small one that fit into one another. The smaller glass is sometimes made of glassware and is referred to as the mixing glass, ideal for stirring a Martini. This version of the cocktail shaker is usually seen at commercial bars, used by professional bartenders, as it is quite user-friendly during busy hours.

Hawthorn Strainer

This is a strainer with a wire spring that fits neatly atop the stainless steel half of a Boston Shaker.

The Blender

Many bars use the kitchen mixer and grinder but that is best for masala grinding. At the bar, use a blender that can even make slush out of ice. Hamilton Beach is a well known brand of bar blenders. Most blended drinks are a mix of more than three ingredients, consisting of juices and complex ingredients.

The Muddler

It can come in plastic or solid wood and is used to extract flavours from fresh ingredients like lemon, mint, grapes, watermelon and other fruits, herbs and vegetables. The muddler helps to prepare the finest Mojitos, Caipiroschkas and Mint Juleps. Just tall enough to stand out of the cocktail shaker and with an approximate diameter of between 1.5-2 inches, this is the magic equipment for modern-day cocktails.

The Bar Spoon

A long handled spoon is used at most bars for mixing and layering drinks. The spoon holds about 5 ml of any liquid and helps to pour ingredients that are measured in dashes. The bar spoon can sometimes be substituted by a stirring rod made of either glass or stainless steel.

Peg Measure or Jigger

This is one of the most essential equipments in a bar. Depending on the weights and measures you prefer, this jigger can come in various volumes of 25 to 30 ml or ounces. A jigger may be two sided or just one sided.

Corkscrew

There are many styles of the corkscrew, from the basic corkscrew with a horizontal wood handle to the wing screw, but the best is called the sommelier's knife or a waiter's friend. This variety of corkscrew has an arm extending to brace against the lip of the bottle for leverage when removing the cork. Some sommelier knives have two steps on the lever and often also a bottle opener. A small-hinged knife blade is concealed in the handle to remove the foil wrapping of wine bottles.

Bottle Openers or Bar Blades

This important and indispensible equipment opens metal cans and caps of fizzy drinks like soda and cola. There is also a different version of a bottle opener used most widely nowadays by bartenders called the Bar Blade which is used to open only bottle caps.

Fruit Juice Extractor or Lemon Squeezer

This is essential for extracting fresh juices and comes in various shapes and sizes. At the bar, this is usually dependent on space provided inside the bar but at home this is a kitchen essential. It can be substituted with a juicer.

Ice Bucket and Ice Tongs

As ice is integral to every drink, it needs to be stored with care. The ice bucket is logically an important requirement for every bar, especially for the bar at home where ice machines may not be available. Ice tongs too, are a must-have.

Knife and a Chopping Board

A sharp knife is best for the bar to cut fruits evenly and straight. A chopping board is essential for cocktail garnish preparation at the bar.

Juices & aerated drinks

Essential mixers that make a bar include juices and aerated waters. Stock up on basic juices such as orange, pineapple, tomato, fresh lemon juice, cranberry, grapefruit and watermelon. Basic fizzy drinks include soda, sparkling water, fresh lime water/soda sweet, cola, tonic, and ginger ale.

Syrups and Mixes

We use various spirits and liqueurs to fix a cocktail and then look into the final finish with regard to dominant flavours and presentation of the drink. All these are then balanced to get what we would probably define as a fine cocktail that has the right mix of everything. Flavours, therefore, rule in a mixed drink and they may come as subtle or very aggressive on both the nose and the palate. Syrups that work well in cocktails are sugar syrup, grenadine syrup and orgeat syrup.

In a mixed drink, we use a wide range of flavours and there is no specific guideline as to what may or may not be used. From fresh ingredients to versatile liqueurs, herbs and vegetables to seasonings used for cooking ~ everything is now kosher in the cocktail world. However, the truth remains that, without a defined flavour, whether strong or mild, we will never be able to define or remember a cocktail. Around the Indian subcontinent, the list of flavours is uncountable but ironically, we cannot use them in our drinks as these seldom exist in liquid form.

Many bartenders make their own mixes. It is easy to prepare, for instance, a Grog Mix (with an Indian touch of cardamom) and a coconut mix (with a packet of Nestlé™ coconut powder). When the Cosmopolitan became popular among consumers, in the absence of cranberry juice, we often used cranberry jelly (cranberry mix with jelly, water and fresh lime juice). Together with the cocktail recipes, we give you a few recipes for making your own mixes for your home bar.

Garnishes

Garnishing a drink can be likened to putting a cherry on a cake. With a little bit of imagination, this final touch to the cocktail can enhance the visual appeal in such a way that even a simple drink can look exotic and refreshing. Anything edible ~ from fresh fruits, vegetables, flowers and candies ~ can be used as garnish. Fresh ingredients such as stuffed olives, cocktail onions, fresh lime, lemon, oranges, mint sprigs, sweet lime, cherries, strawberries, celery, cucumber, pineapple, orchid, rose & marigold petals make great garnishes.

Condiments and Bitters

The list includes bitters, powdered sugar, caramelised grain sugar, salt, pepper, Tabasco sauce, Worcestershire sauce, milk, single cream, eggs, nutmeg powder and cinnamon sticks.

As the name suggests, bitters are bitter in taste. The origin of bitters is probably linked to herbal medicine, when spirits of all types were being flavoured with herbs, roots, fruit peels or bark of trees that were considered to have healing properties. One of the facts that support this is the invention of tonic water. In the past, tonic water was consumed as a pick-me-up with a strong dose of quinine. Today's version is a sweeter one. Bitters today come in various styles, ranging from Campari and Fernet Branca (Italy) or Unicum (Hungary) that are consumed in a manner similar to spirits, to strong bitters such as Angostura (Trinidad and Tobago) and Underberg (Germany) that are used to add flavour to the drink. Some bitters are also used in the kitchen to add flavour to meat.

Of the many bitters that we see today, the most popular is the Angostura bitters which were invented by a German doctor in Venezuela, who had been serving the South American revolutionary, Simon Bolivar. Today, the distillery is in Trinidad.

A preference for bitters is an acquired taste that only develops with time as the palate matures. Liqueurs and syrups win over bitters as the preferred flavouring for cocktails ~ clearly, not many people have the gall to experience a bitter-tasting drink!

Bitters have made a comeback in recent times, especially among health conscious consumers, with new cocktail recipes where bartenders have moved away from traditional sweet flavours to the dry style of mixing drinks. Professional bartenders are also inventing their own bitters with flavours such as chocolate and coffee, to enhance the taste of their cocktails and make them unique.

What comes in various shapes and sizes and holds both the sweet and the dry?

What is sometimes long and sometimes very short and yet suits every lip?

Got you thinking, didn't we?

Glassware comes in different designs, shapes and volumes. Without the glass or the cup, the drink that we consider elegant and soothing would certainly have had neither the charm nor be appreciated the way it is today. All glassware for drinks should preferably be transparent, to best enjoy the drink in its true colours. Glassware at the bar can be divided into two major categories ~ flatware and stemware. The basic difference between the two categories is the use of ice. In most cases, straight drinks (like spirits, wine and beer without a mixer) which include ice could be served in flatware while stemware would not be appropriate for drinks with ice.

Glassware {Flatware}

Highball

This is usually a tall glass with an approximate volume of about 250-300 ml of any liquid. This is used to serve most simple drinks, both alcoholic and non-alcoholic. The name of the glass is derived from the usage of serving most highball drinks, like vodka tonics and gin tonics, in it.

Old Fashioned or Rocks Glass

This is a short, fat glass with an approximate volume of 350-400 ml and is used to serve most spirit on the rocks. Some famous cocktails like Old Fashioned (from where it got its name), Manhattan and Rusty Nail are always served in this glass.

Tall Collins

This is a tall glass, taller than the highball and with a much larger volume, between 350-400 ml. It gets its name from the cocktail Tom Collins and is the classic glass for most drinks that have a double measure.

Tall Zombie

This is the tallest of cylindrical glassware. Taller than the Collins, this glass is synonymous with Long Island Iced Tea and Blue Lagoon cocktails. Most tall cocktails with aerated water are best served in the zombie glass.

Pilsner Glass

A tall conical glass with a narrow base and a wide opening, this glass is used to serve lager beers. The name is derived from the popular light lager beer Pilsner and the glass comes in various volumes ranging from 200 ml-400 ml.

Shot Glass

This is usually a straight glass with a volume of about 60 ml or 90 ml. In appearance, this could be the youngest brother of the highball. This glass is usually for shots and shooters ~ cocktails that come in small measures of 60 or 75 ml and are consumed in a single gulp.

Glassware {Stemware}

Martini Glass

Traditionally, this is a cocktail glass with a smaller volume, approximately 100 ml, used for most old style cocktails such as the classic Dry Martini, Side Car, Between the Sheets and Pink Gin. It is a tall stemmed, V-shaped glass where most straight up cocktails could be served.

Coupé

Once used for serving sweeter versions of champagne, this stemmed glass owes its origins to seventeenth century England and continued to be popularly used for serving champagne and sparkling wines in the 1930s. The coupé has a wide opening and is used today for serving classic straight up drinks instead of champagne.

A few good examples

White Wine Glass

This is a simpler form of the wine glass simply because the white wine category is not as complex as the reds. It has a long stem and a bowl that is not too bulging. This glass has a narrower top and eases the flavours. The approximate volume of this glass varies between 180 ml-300 ml, based on the height of the stem.

Red Wine Glass

This glass could come in more than one variety and in the glassware category it is the widest of all. Usually it comes with the traditional tall stem with a rounded bowl and a smaller opening which helps the flavours to concentrate. This allows one to best enjoy the complex aromas of the wine. This glass would have various shapes apart from the all-purpose red wine glass and is totally based on the wine, the region and its character.

Champagne Flute

This is a tall, very narrow-stemmed glass with a small bowl. It is a specially designed sleek narrow glass for champagnes and sparkling wines and is best used to retain the carbonation of the drink for a longer period of time because of its minimal surface area.

A hard-core spiritualist would probably be quite finicky about glassware, with every good reason ~ the right kind enhances the character of your drink. But we always encourage our friends to experiment with glasses and mugs that are traditionally not meant for alcoholic beverages. Try serving your cocktails in a chai glass ~ Indian variations of classic cocktails work quite well and add to the appeal of the drink if presented right. Terracotta cups that impart an aroma and sweetness of clay to your drink go well with cocktails that have milk or cream ~ the Panchamrita (see page 126) can easily be served that way. Don't make the mistake of serving alcohol in steel glasses. It just doesn't work and kills the pleasure of drinking altogether. Remember, drinking is as much about seeing the concoction as tasting it.

Brandy Balloon or Snifter

This is a globular glass with a very narrow top, used to serve the finest brandies aged for a certain period of time. The short stem helps in passing on the warmth from the palm into the spirit and releases the delicate aromas. The narrow top allows the flavours to concentrate so that it can be best sniffed and enjoyed by the consumer.

Beer Goblet

Also called a chalice, it has a short stem with a big bowl and is slightly narrow at the top. It is largely used in commercial establishments to serve almost all styles of beer. These glasses also vary with country of origin of beer, character, style and history. Whatever the style of the glass, the volume of the beer goblets is above 400 ml.

Liqueur Glass

This is a short-stemmed glass with a very small volume, 45-75 ml, for serving liqueurs after dinner. The bowl of the glass comes in many shapes.

Sherry Glass

A short-stemmed glass, slightly larger in volume compared to a liqueur glass, this glass is best used to serve sherry or any other aperitif, aromatised or fortified wines.

Aperitif Glass

This is another classic stemmed glass that is used to serve lesser volumes of alcohol. It is used widely in bars to serve Sherry and Port and cocktails such as Sazerac. Many innovations also go well with this classic stemware.

Bar Checklist

TOOLS
- Bottle opener
- Corkscrew
- Muddler
- Strainer
- Cocktail shaker
- Lemon squeezer
- Bar spoon
- Peg measure
- Pourer

APPLIANCES
- Refrigerator
- Blender
- Ice crusher

ICE AND WATER

SYRUPS AND MIXES

AERATED DRINKS
- Soda
- Tonic water
- Cola
- Fresh lime water/soda sweet
- Energy drinks

JUICES

BITTERS

CONDIMENTS

GARNISHES

GLASSWARE
- Wine glasses
- Old fashioned/rocks glasses
- Tall glasses
- Mugs/Pilsners/goblets (for beer)
- Shot glasses

EXTRAS
- Stirrers
- Straws
- Napkins
- Toothpicks
- Cocktail swords

Stocking up

If you are well stocked for your kitchen, it is likely that you are equipped for your home bar. We have always found the best ingredients by wandering around markets, taking in the sights and smells from the food and vegetable stalls and drawing inspiration for innovative cocktails from what we would put in our food. What works in your food is likely to impart an interesting flavour to your drink. What you would normally use to marinate your meat could possibly provide a decent finish to a Martini. Who knows? We encourage our friends to innovate ~ use curry leaves and herbs such as basil and coriander to infuse your alcohol. Garnish the cocktail with fresh fruits, petals ~ rose and marigold work quite well ~ and herbs. Spice it up with peppercorns or cinnamon. Explore your markets and see what could work. Visit departmental stores, you may find a version of marmalade that could add that extra something to a frozen Daiquiri. Don't be afraid to experiment.

If you travel frequently, think beyond the Scotch at the duty-free store. Try stocking up on Japanese whiskies or even Bourbons. The latter make an excellent base for cocktails. Invest in Jamaican rum or even Mauritian rhum agricole that is often infused with vanilla, coffee or spices. Purchase Ouzo if you are travelling to Greece. Or its cousin, Raki, in Turkey. Limoncello, if you happen to be in Italy. Borovička if your travels take you to Slovakia. It tastes quite good with fresh rhododendron juice from the Himalayas. Who would know that unless one tried? Try Tuica if you're in Romania. It is vile but worth experimenting with. Sake if you're in Japan.

Nothing beats good research ~ we have a range of books and information on bartending, cocktail recipes and alcohol and we scour the internet for ideas. If you are passionate about something, there's nothing to hold you back from knowing and experimenting, is there?

Know your Poison

OFFICIAL BARTENDER'S AND PARTY GUIDE
DER'S
AR
RGOTTEN COCKTAILS
Ted Haigh AKA Dr. Cocktail
QUARRY
CHRONICLE BOOKS
KATE WHITEMAN
MAGGIE MAYHEW
XOLOGY
POTTER
TILL LIFE
WILEY
ASY
DIAGEO RESERVE 2010
A LIQUID HISTORY
he Classic Malts of Scotland
Jason Lowe
MITCHELL BEAZLEY
WALLER POND
A GUIDE TO BAR FOOD AND COCKTAIL PARTY FARE
drink·ol·o·gy
EAMES
SECRET LIFE OF B
GREAT B
BIZOLOGY
COCKTAILS, CULTURE, AND A GUIDE TO
THE organic beer
KARL PETZKE
TEQUILA
THE LITTLE BOOK OF Whisky
Laurence Kretchmer
GUIDE TO
ALBERTO RUY SÁNCHEZ and MARGARITA de ORELLANA
TEQU
THE COMPLETE ENCYCLOPEDIA
BEER
WYBOROWA BARTENDE
André Dominé
The Ultimat
BA
BOOK
DRI
THE WORLD ATLAS OF
WHISK

We Indians love whisky, especially when it's on the rocks. Many warm Indian summers ago, we thought of initiating a friend in red wine. A very good bottle of Chianti was procured and the initiation was underway. Our friend looked longingly at the deep red liquid ~ a full-bodied wine danced inside the ample globe of a wine glass. We toasted and sipped. All round the table, appreciative murmurs were heard. Our friend too, politely nodded in approval. 'Nice drink,' he said, summoning the waiter. 'I need ice. This is not cold enough. I have my whisky on the rocks, why not wine on the rocks?' he added with a smile.

Initiation in new and different kinds of alcohol requires an open mind ~ one that does not unconsciously compare the drink with a previous experience. With due apologies to the Scots and the Irish ~ whisky is had on the rocks in India because of the climate but wine on the rocks? When trying an alcoholic beverage for the first time, we suggest you first try it as it is traditionally consumed. Make your drinking experience meaningful. Encourage your sensory perceptions to participate as much as your taste buds. Observe the fluid in its glass. Smell the drink as it stands before you. Bury your nose, if you will. Keep your eyes closed and let your nose explore the liquid. You will find that it talks back to you. It is the smell that gives your taste buds a heads-up of what is to follow. When you clink your glass and raise a toast, you allow your ears to participate in this pleasure of drinking. Now sip the drink, slowly and smoothly. Allow your taste buds to respond. Never gulp ~ that is disrespecting the spirit. Savour the alcohol and understand its flavours and distinctiveness. This will help you understand how best to use a certain kind of alcohol as a base for your cocktails.

To help you know your poison better, we introduce to you, a few characters who will play an important role in defining the cocktail experience throughout the book ~ Whisky, Rum, Vodka, Gin and Brandy. Supporting them in their roles are Tequila and liqueurs. A few Indian country spirits also make brief appearances. Playing a very important role in helping you enjoy the cocktail experience, are water and ice.

Whisky

Whisky consumers are so loyal to its flavour, versatility and style that many women would find such steadfastness enviable. It is distilled from cereal grains ~ barley, wheat, rye and corn and has to be matured over a period of time in oak barrels. Malt whisky is, at most times, more full-bodied and pungent as compared to the grain version, which is lighter in taste and character. Though prepared in a distillery, whisky gets its character from its wooden barrel during maturation.

Although whisky is made all over the world, by whisky we usually refer to Scotch and Irish ~ the Gaelic for whisky is an unpronounceable 'Usque Baugh' or 'Usque Beatha'. Scotch comes in two major styles, malts and blended. Malt whiskies are made from malted barley and come from a single distillery, for instance Glenfiddich, Glenlivet and Laphroaig. Blended Scotch is usually a blend of malt and grain whiskies like Johnnie Walker, Chivas Regal, Black Dog and Teachers. The Scots often say the real way to drink a scotch is with a splash of water. How much is a splash? Well, maybe equal parts, but what about ice? The Scots sip the spirit without ice. For us folks living in the tropics, ice is a blessing.

Because of its character with regard to colour, aroma and taste, whisky is not a popular base for mixing cocktails. To fix a good whisky cocktail, one needs to know the spirit well enough to compliment its character with ingredients and mixers that suit it best.

American whiskies or Bourbons are also popular. Classic cocktails such as Whisky Sour and Manhattan are prepared mostly with American whiskey and not Scotch. This is because of the character of American whiskies and the sweet notes they possess. Scotch, on the other hand, does not feature as the base for many cocktails simply because of its style, which does not do justice to a bartender's imagination. The Rusty Nail and Rob Roy are not as popular as the Whisky Sour.

TOP WHISKY COCKTAILS

Manhattan (see page 42)

Whisky Sour (see page 72)

Old Fashioned (see page 46)

Mint Julep (see page 48)

Rob Roy (see page 42)

O' Soma (see page 134)

Always ~ Use a silent mix such as water, soda or ice.

Innovate with green or white tea.

Never ~ Mix whisky with a citrus, including fresh lime water/soda sweet.

Rum

One of the oldest spirits known to man, rum is the sweetest spirit base for a cocktail and a favourite with many bartenders. No other spirit has played such an inspiring role in history. From the rough drink of seamen and pirates, revolution and war, colonialism and slavery, rum has evolved as the spirit of relaxation, a spirit that is easy yet complex, a popular spirit at the well of every bar across the globe.

Rum is associated with the production of sugar. Ten thousand years ago, sugarcane cultivation spread from the islands of Indonesia to China and India. The Vedas, that date to 2000 BC, mention two intoxicant drinks attributed with mythical powers, Siddu derived from sugarcane juice and Gaudi extracted from molasses ~ the brown sticky by-product of sugar. In the present context, 'Rum Agricole' is similar to Siddu and 'Rum Industrial' akin to Gaudi. Rum became a more defined drink during the sixteenth century. As sugarcane became the main Caribbean crop and molasses a readily available resource after the production of sugar, rum came to be called the 'kill devil' for its fearsome reputation and rejoicing behaviour of slaves after the drink.

Rum supposedly has more than five hundred characteristics and this makes it versatile from every aspect of the spirit, whether light or full-bodied. It comes in various styles, from a light version to more rich and complex aged rums with characters that could beat any other spirit. With its mystical character, sweetness and alcohol strength, this spirit is certainly a great base for a cocktail.

Rum varieties range from light style rums that are colourless and charcoal filtered, to the gold coloured mellow and matured rum, where the colour and the character is achieved through many years of aging in oak barrels. Dark or black rums are flavoured with caramel after being aged for several years. However, the best rums are always golden in colour and could be as young as a three-year-old to as old as thirty years.

TOP RUM COCKTAILS

Mai Tai (see page 44)

The Daiquiri (see page 66)

Mojito (see page 52)

Southern Somras (see page 112)

A very versatile spirit, one can easily experiment and innovate with rum. Feel free to let your creative juices flow!

Brandy

This golden brown spirit derives its name from the Dutch word Brandewijn, that means burnt wine. Brandy is prepared from fruits that have a high sugar content ~ apple, cherry, apricot and pear ~ and the process involves fermentation, distillation and aging. Maturation in oak casks gives this spirit its character while the colour is derived from caramel.

This spirit was invented by monks and Moorish scholars who pioneered the art of distillation at a time when Europe was only familiar with the process of fermentation and was therefore limited to preparing wine from grapes. The most popular style of brandy comes from the Cognac and Armagnac region of France. Spanish brandies are also quite popular. It is believed that the first brandy was prepared in the city of Jerez by the Moors who brought the stills and started distilling wine.

Cognac is considered the finest of brandies available and is still distilled in an alambic charentais or a traditional pot. What makes it so special is the terroir, the French word for soil. But it encompasses more than soil ~ climate and the impact of the sun on the vine is just as important. Cognac can be aged from two years to as many as forty years. The process of aging is a closely guarded secret as well as a rather complex one. Cognac is classified by age as follows: VS (Very Special) for a minimum of two years, VSOP (Very Special Old Pale) for a minimum of six years and XO (Extra Old) for a minimum of eight years. Some well-known Cognac brands are Martell, Remy Martin, Hennessy, Courvoisier and Hine.

Armagnac, though not as popular as Cognac, was distilled even before the latter. Cognac's popularity is attributed to the proximity of the region to the sea, which made it easy for the spirit to travel. Armagnac is distilled in alambic armagnacais or column stills, although these days the old style pot stills are also used. Armagnac can be produced from twelve varieties of grapes and is classified in a manner similar to Cognac. When Cognacs and Armagnacs are aged over forty years, they are stored in special glass jars to avoid over aging. These are known as Paridis. Some well-known Argmanacs are Janneau & Tariquet.

The Dutch shipped Spanish brandies and popularised them, although it was a low quality wine that was distilled to produce these brandies. The solera system of fractional blending makes these brandies unique ~ here the spirit is blended with brandies of various ages.

Brandies like Cognac, Armagnac and Spanish brandies are categorised as luxury spirits. Popular as an after dinner drink, they are best consumed neat without a mixer. They can also be savoured with water, warm water, tonic, soda or ginger ale. Brandy is also considered an elixir for the winter chill because of its warm character.

TOP BRANDY COCKTAILS

Gold Stinger (see page 142)

Corpse Reviver (see page 64)

Cognac & Chai (see page 108)

Fine cognac or brandies should ideally be savoured neat or with a silent chaser such as soda, tonic or ginger ale. Cocktails featuring brandy are extremely rare and we recommend you know the spirit well before you experiment.

Gin

Originally distilled for medicinal purposes by a Dutch physician called Dr Franciscus Sylvius, gin was prepared from Juniper berries. Developed to cure kidney ailments, it was adopted by the English over time. The name gin is derived from the Dutch (Genever) and French (Genievre) names for Juniper. Gin is obtained from the re-distillation of a high proof distillate with Juniper, caraway, coriander, lemon or orange peel.

The formula for distilling gin was picked up by English soldiers in Holland fighting the Spanish during the Eight Years' War. Gin's popularity in England was chiefly due to the high taxes imposed by the government on other spirits. A drink of the working class, gin could be prepared quite cheaply with low quality ingredients. Often called 'mothers ruin', gin was associated with the youth who often lost their lives consuming the cheaper version of this spirit.

Although predominantly flavoured with juniper berries, distillers today balance the flavour of gin with botanicals such as coriander, caraway, cassia bark or citrus fruit peels. The most popular style of gin is the London Dry Gin, which is dry and not sweet as compared to the traditional gin from Holland.

G&T or gin and tonic, the most favoured gin-based cocktail, owes its origin to India. The soldiers of the British East India Company consumed tonic water with quinine, a rather bitter mixture as a cure and preventive to malaria. Gin was added to reduce the bitterness of the drink, thus resulting in the birth of one of the most popular cocktails in the world.

TOP GIN COCKTAILS

Dry Martini (see page 56)

Gin and Tonic (see page 74)

Summer Citrus (see page 94)

Ananda (see page 110)

Remember ~ Gin is best mixed with light aerated beverages such as ginger ale, tonic or fresh lime water/soda sweet.

Never ~ Mix gin with colas or use juices, except lemon, to fix gin-based cocktails.

Vodka

The word vodka is derived from the word for water, which in Russian is voda and in Polish is woda. The raw material for vodka must contain starch and can range from cereal grains such as rye, sweet fruits, tubers and roots such as potatoes or molasses. Fermented alcoholic wash from these raw materials is distilled in old (pot) or new (patent) still distillation process to produce a colourless spirit that is high in alcohol content and low in character.

Filtration is an important stage in vodka production as this removes all unwanted flavours that could be present in the spirit even after multiple distillations. The challenge for most vodka producers is to be able to eliminate any hint of distinctiveness of its base ingredients used and thus the many techniques involved in its production process. Filtration involves use of charcoal derived from different wood varieties depending on the production house, which also enhances the character of vodka.

Water and the minerals present in it define the character of the vodka. Old style vodkas were defined by the harsh bite of alcohol in the mouth and aftertaste. Today, most vodka distillers emphasise on the mineral content of water, its source, raw material used and finally the number of times the spirit is distilled and filtered.

Vodka is best enjoyed when consumed neat (chilled), with lots of ice and a twist or with mixers of any type. Fine vodkas are a popular base for Martinis in many bars.

TOP VODKA COCKTAILS

Martini (see page 56)

Salty Dog (see page 82)

Orange Caipiroschka (see page 88)

Always ~ Consume a fine vodka neat or on the rocks.

Never ~ Underestimate vodka. A silent spirit, it goes down very quickly and can give you the worst hangovers.

Tequila

The Aztecs believed that lightning struck an agave and set its heart on fire. The wonderful nectar that remained within its heart would later be transformed into Tequila ~ the national drink of Mexico. Considered a gift of the gods, agave is a versatile plant that is eaten as fruit, has medicinal properties, is used to produce yarn and in construction. The Aztecs fermented its juice to make an intoxicating drink called Pulque that was believed to have mythical powers, as its consumption took them closer to God. The Spaniards, who conquered Mexico in 1521, brought with them the technique of distillation. They transformed this traditional alcohol and Tequila or Mezcal was born.

Various methods can be employed to produce different forms of Tequila ~ the commonest being 100 per cent Tequila and Mixto. The 100 per cent Tequila uses only 100 per cent blue agave while a Mixto uses 49 per cent sugar extracted from other raw materials to produce the same, thus reducing the cost of production. The usual distillation of Tequila happens in two cycles, the first distillate at approximately 30 per cent alcohol by volume is called Ordinario while the second distillate at approximately 55 per cent alcohol by volume is referred to as Tequila. Modern-day distillers distil more than twice to produce a much mellower version of the spirit with higher alcohol content. This is later reduced to a drinkable strength of 40 per cent alcohol by volume.

The Norma Official Mexicana prescribes laws and regulations that determine the production and quality of Tequila. The term Tequila can only be given to spirit produced in the state of Jalisco and the neighbouring states of Guanajuato, Nayarit, Michoacan and Tamaulipas in the Gulf of Mexico. Spirits from other states are referred to as Mezcal.

Tequila is considered to be a drink that can be consumed in a single gulp ~ lick, bite and shoot. This was the case for the silver or gold Tequilas and can be acceptable to the reposado depending upon its smoothness on the palate. New age Tequilas (anejo or extra anejo), however, are the sipping spirits best enjoyed neat, with ice or a chaser as a short or a long drink. These Tequilas derive character from several years of maturation like other matured spirits and are smoother and easier on the palate.

Common Tequila myths

Tequila drinking happens on 'wild nights'.

Tequila tastes horrible.

You can only do Tequila shots.

Tequila is made from cactus.

Tequila will make you sick the next day.

TOP TEQUILA COCKTAILS

Frozen Lemon Margarita (see page 58)

A versatile drink, Tequila suits every drinking mood and works just as well as a frozen cocktail or as shots. Fine Tequila can be sipped neat or with ice.

Liqueurs, cordials or digestives

The word liqueur comes from the Latin word liquefacere, which means to drip/drop or extract. In layperson's language, a liqueur is sweetened alcohol. Technically, for any spirit to be classified as a liqueur, it must have at least 100 gm of sugar per litre and a minimum alcohol content of 15 per cent.

During the Middle Ages, monks would grow herbs and medicinal plants and use their extracts to treat various illnesses. As most of these extracts were preserved in alcohol and would consequently become quite bitter, it was customary to add sugar to sweeten the concoction. However, sugar was an expensive commodity and the liqueurs prepared during those days were beyond the reach of the common man. However, small doses of liqueur were often prescribed to treat the sick. These medicinal liqueurs were mostly derived from herbs.

Liqueurs are extensively used in bars as cocktail flavouring and those such as Cointreau and Triple Sec are used to bind a cocktail together. Cream and coffee liqueurs such as Baileys and Kahlua are popular.

TOP COCKTAILS

Margarita (see page 56)

Cosmopolitan (see page 70)

Cold Coffee Cocktail (see page 140)

Always ~ Use a glass of small volume such as an aperitif glass to serve liqueurs.

Never ~ Serve liqueurs before dinner or a fine meal.

Fine liqueurs are best consumed neat. However, fixing cocktails featuring liqueurs, it is important to balance their sweetness.

Going local {Chhang, Raksi, Mahua, Feni}

The Himalayan belt, ranging from Ladakh, Nepal and the states of northeast India, have for generations, brewed and distilled alcohol in various styles using raw materials such as rice, millets, rhododendrons and molasses. It was the extreme cold in these mountainous locales that prompted households to produce alcohol. Alcohol is thus part of local custom and integral to people's dietary habits.

Chhang is a Tibetan word for fermented rice or millet beer. The Nepalese call this Jhaar (pronounced with a nasal intonation) and a stronger version of this is Nigar—a drink not meant for the faint hearted. Chhang is prepared from boiled rice (in some parts of lower Darjeeling, tapioca root is boiled and fermented during the winter) that is allowed to ferment in an airtight container over seven days with the aid of dried yeast (*morcha*). The light yellow liquid accumulated during the fermentation process is called the Nigar, potent and full-bodied to smell and taste. The rest of the brew that is primarily rice paste, is pressed against a V-shaped strainer to prepare the less potent Chhang, which has a creamy texture. The beverage has a sweet aroma upon fermentation, but its taste depends on the quality of raw material used. It can therefore be sour, medium dry or sweet (though not quite like a liqueur).

Raksi is popular in Nepal and the Darjeeling hills in India. It is a generic name given to any spirit distilled in the region from molasses or other grains.

Mahua is a spirit produced by tribal people living amid the dense forests in the heart of India. It is as cloudy as lemonade but rather harsh to taste. Distilled without filtration or clarification, this drink is extracted from the flower, fruit and seed of the Mahua (bassialatifolia) tree. The fruit of the Mahua ripens towards the end of summer. Replete with nectar, the fruit is harvested and hand pressed to extract juice. Fermentation takes place in the open over two days. The beverage is then distilled in clay pots. Groundwater is used to distil the alcohol and it is the water that lends character to this spirit.

Feni, a spirit from Goa, is attributed to coconut or cashew. Extremely pungent, the spirit is distilled three times. When distilled once, it is referred to as Urrack, which has less alcohol content but a more pungent and aggressive flavour and taste. Of all native spirits in India, Feni is the only one that is bottled. Recent innovations at improving the taste of Feni involve maturing the beverage to smoothen the flavour so it can be savoured without mixing. If you do have a bottle of Feni at home, we encourage you to fix Mumbai Slurp ~ a cocktail that we have innovated (see page 120).

Water on the side

Never underestimate what you get for free. Water ~ natural, free flowing, tasteless and colourless ~ is a gift that we often take for granted. Keeping yourself hydrated when you drink alcohol will not dilute the effects of the spirit, but it will help your body to cope with the alcohol and reduce the chances of a hangover the following morning. Water in the body slows down absorption of alcohol. Water is the ultimate cleanser ~ make sure it is by your side when you order yourself a cocktail.

Drinking water throughout the night along with alcohol also ensures you drink responsibly. So, when attending a party or while entertaining, play the perfect host and offer your guests sufficient water to enjoy and sample your cocktail creations. The cocktail experience should be enjoyable till the end, irrespective of what we drink.

Although many good bars always serve you drinks with a glass of water on the side, this is yet to become part of the bartender's discipline in India. While it is important that the customer drinks, it is equally important that the experience doesn't make him sick. Water on the side is exactly that lifeline.

Ice, ice baby

A cocktail is incomplete without ice. There are a few hot drinks that obviously do not require ice ~ Hot Toddy, for instance ~ but imagine mixing a drink without ice.

Ice is the backbone of any bar. Available as cubes, crushed, shaved or in nuggets, not only does ice help in mixing, shaking or blending a drink, it also adds to its visual appeal. Cashing in on what aesthetics can do to a drink, Japanese bartenders now carve ice before the customer and shape it into a ball. The Japanese ice ball is the new serving style in many bars where spirits are accompanied with an ice ball rather the traditional 'on the rocks'.

Ice enhances the taste of a drink. It smoothens the spirit and makes it less harsh on the palate. On the other hand, too much ice can also numb tastebuds, thus killing the pleasure of enjoying a spirit with character.

Depending on whether the consumer wishes to taste alcohol or flavours in a cocktail, a skilful bartender can vary the amount of ice to fix a drink that would suit him. The classic Martini, one of the strongest cocktails, for instance, is served cold as it is an almost pure spirit served straight. We must ensure therefore, that we stir with loads of ice in a mixing glass to ensure that there is less melting and dilution but more chillness to the cocktail. The chill from the ice ensures that the delicate flavours of the vermouth stand out and the harsh character of the spirit is reduced. A good Martini requires that the ice be washed so that the flavours of a hard cocktail can be enjoyed.

On the other hand, adding ice to a smooth, peaty single malt can ruin the experience of drinking an aged whisky. With most fine sipping spirits, that have distinct flavours and character, it is best to forgo the ice. Light spirits or those that can be mixed, work very well when ice is added.

Measure for measure!

A good drink is measured correctly and balanced with other ingredients to get a consistent flavour that defines it as a Martini, a Mojito or a Bloody Mary. A standard recipe that specifies the amount of alcohol that should go into a drink sets the benchmark around which you can experiment or innovate ~ if you prefer to taste less alcohol, reduce the quantity or balance it with a non-alcoholic mix or ice. In bars, standard measures may vary, some have 45 ml as the standard measure of alcohol in a drink while others have 60 ml. Based upon this measure, we can adjust the amount of alcohol that goes into the cocktail. For instance, the specified alcohol content in a Margarita is 60 ml, that can either have 45 ml Tequila and 15 ml Cointreau or 30 ml Tequila and 30 ml Cointreau.

For the bartender, standard measures help him to work out costs and calculate sales against consumption.

Cocktail making techniques

To fix a good cocktail, it is important to know alcohol. Every spirit has its own character and taste. You also need a certain amount of imagination and creativity. Knowing what ingredients ~ other than alcohol ~ will go into the cocktail is also important. Before fixing the drink, you should mentally know how the cocktail would taste and look. Everything else depends upon technique, skill and presentation. Here, we list a few cocktail making techniques that go into creating that perfect drink.

Stir

Muddle

Stir

A drink is stirred when you want a drink that is cold, or on the stronger side but want to minimise the harshness of alcohol. We also stir when the ingredients used are just two or three and are alcoholic in nature and when the flavours are delicate and sensitive. A good example of a stirred drink is the classic Martini.

Shake

Shaking is vigorous mixing. Shake it hard; shake it with style, long shake or short shake. A cocktail is shaken depending on its ingredients. Shaking helps to break the ice, mix complex ingredients together and cool the drink. The quality of ice is of foremost importance while shaking a drink. Flaky soft ice results in a watery drink. The ice used in the shaking process must be hard ~ solid cube or round ice ~ and clear. Not all drinks require ice for shaking; for instance, while preparing a Whisky Sour we shake all ingredients without ice so that the egg white does not coagulate. Ice would defeat the purpose. This is called a dry shake.

Blend

You blend drinks either when the fluids involved are too complex or when the cocktail recipe contains too many ingredients. Needless to say, you use a blender for the process. In most cases, ice is involved in the process of blending a drink. A short blend is when the only intention is to break the ice. A long blend, on the other hand, is when the ingredients need to fuse into one another to lend character to the cocktail. Piña Colada is a cocktail that requires blending.

Muddle

This involves the extraction of flavours from fresh ingredients by the application of force in a manner similar to that of a mortar and pestle. Vary the pressure according to the nature of ingredients ~ for instance, herbs need gentle muddling whereas fresh fruits and peels require hard muddling. Likewise, spices require a bit of strength to be cracked to release flavours. Muddling is integral to a Mojito.

Straining

Most cocktails are strained as they are poured. A hawthorn or julep strainer is commonly used for this purpose. There chief reason for straining is to hold the ice back after mixing the drink. Ice is required to cool the drink down and too much ice tends to water it down. Other reasons why one would strain a drink would be to avoid fruit pulp and pips (for cocktails that use fresh ingredients), avoid small flakes of ice, and to obtain a clear drink.

Strain

Pour

A built drink is one where the preparation involves pouring ingredients over lots of ice in a standard format. Tom Collins is a drink that is built over lots of ice. A stirrer is always provided to mix the drink and enjoy its unique flavours.

A layered drink is where every ingredient is allowed to float on one another depending upon its density. B-52 and Flatliner are examples of layered drinks.

Pouring

Pouring is critical to the cocktail making process. Pouring is usually done with the help of a peg measure (jigger) to maintain consistency and control of the drink. Some bartenders practice free pouring while preparing a cocktail but that is only possible when one has an experienced hand.

Cocktail Families

Collins

A Collins usually has fresh lime juice, sugar syrup and sparkling water or soda, with a base spirit (gin, whisky, brandy, vodka). These cocktails are always prepared over ice in the built up style e.g. Tom Collins, John Collins.

Flips

These are drinks that always have egg yolk and are shaken e.g. Sherry Flip, Port Flip.

Sours

Drinks that have egg white, fresh lime juice and sugar syrup as chief ingredients, with an alcohol base e.g. Whisky Sour or Amaretto Sour.

Fizz

A drink with egg white and always topped with aerated water e.g. Gin Fizz.

Colada

A drink that always has a coconut and pineapple base and is always blended e.g. Piña Colada.

Frozen drinks

Slushy drinks with a standard recipe and usually blended with lots of cube and crushed ice e.g. Frozen Margarita or Daiquiri.

Dessert drinks

Drinks that have creamy liqueur as their base e.g. King Alfonso (Kahlua with cream).

Hot winter drinks

These are always served hot and may have soup, stock or hot coffee and tea as a chief ingredient, with an alcohol base e.g. Irish Coffees.

Shots and shooters

These drinks are served in a shot or a shooter glass straight up and can be layered, shaken or stirred. The prescribed way of consuming these drinks is in a single gulp e.g. Kamikaze or Slippery Nipple.

Cocktails *& Dreams*

Recipes ~ Classics

Cocktails that are considered classics were probably invented by bartenders on the request of a customer who wanted to taste something out of the ordinary. The concoction may have worked with a few clients thereafter and became the signature drink of that bar. These cocktails travelled from one bar to another and indeed, from one city to the next, thus colonising the bar scene the world over. Although these cocktails have a standard recipe, bartenders often give their own twist or vary the measures according to customer preferences. The base and the mixer however, remain the same. Often, classic cocktails spark debates on how they were named, the way in which they are mixed and so on. However, all classics have history and a very convincing story of how they were invented. Sometimes, historical events have resulted in the birth of a classic. A good example is the Cuba Libre that is attributed to the Cuban war of independence. The Rob Roy is associated with Scottish hero, Robert Roy MacGregor. In short, a classic has pedigree.

Popular culture ~ cinema and TV ~ has popularised certain cocktails. The secret agent, James Bond, has done much for the Vodkatini with his bar call, 'Give me a Vodka Martini shaken, not stirred'. The HBO series, *Sex and the City*, similarly reinvented the Cosmopolitan as a drink of hip, urban women. Prominent liquor companies have aggressively marketed certain spirits as a cocktail base and even patented recipes and thus contributed to classics going global. Classics are easy to fix because they are de rigueur for a bartender and suit the palate of the average consumer.

Manhattan

The Manhattan can come in various forms, sweet (as mentioned here) or dry (by replacing the sweet vermouth with dry vermouth) or at times can be perfect (equal parts of both sweet and dry vermouth). It can also be served straight (without ice) or on the rocks.

Ingredients

American whiskey	45 ml
Sweet vermouth	15 ml
Aromatic bitters	2 dashes

Method

In an old fashioned glass filled with cube ice, pour the ingredients. Stir and serve with fresh cherry as garnish.

Preparation time ~ 2 minutes | Rating ~ Easy

Rob Roy: This variation of the Manhattan was invented in 1894 at the Waldrof hotel in New York. Named after the Scottish folk hero, Robert Roy MacGregor, this cocktail uses blended Scotch as its base spirit. Every other ingredient in the drink is the same and the cocktail can be served dry, sweet, perfect, straight, or on the rocks.

Mai Tai

This drink originated in Tahiti. When it was first served, the patron who savoured it called it Mai Tai Roa Ae which means 'out of the world, the best'. There are many recipes for the Mai Tai ~ the recipe below is from an old-school bartender and was one of the most successful rum cocktails during my Polo Lounge days.

Ingredients

Aged or gold rum	40 ml
Orange liqueur	10 ml
Amaretto	10 ml
Orange juice	45 ml
Pineapple juice	45 ml
Fresh lime juice	15 ml

Method

Add the ingredients in a cocktail shaker filled with ice and shake well. Pour into a rocks glass along with the ice. Garnish with any citrus fruit wedge and serve.

Preparation time ~ 4 minutes | Rating ~ Difficult

Old Fashioned

Ingredients

American whiskey	55 ml
Sugar cube	1
Aromatic bitters	2 dashes

Method

In an old fashioned glass, drop the sugar cube, aromatic bitters and 30 ml American whiskey. Stir until the sugar is dissolved. Fill the glass with ice and pour the remaining whisky. Stir, garnish with orange peel and serve.

Preparation time ~ 3 minutes | Rating ~ Easy

The Old Fashioned need not be made with just American whiskey. Use the above recipe with any mature spirit with character such as rum, cognac or brandy, aged Tequilas or whiskies.

Mint Julep

Ingredients

American whiskey	60 ml
Fresh mint	20-30 leaves
Sugar	1 tsp
Water/ginger ale/soda	Optional

Method

In a whiskey tumbler, muddle the mint leaves and sugar.
Fill with crushed ice and pour the American whiskey. Mix well.
Top with water or ginger ale or soda (optional), garnish with a mint sprig and serve.

Preparation time ~ 5 minutes | Rating ~ Medium

Sangria

Ingredients (serves 5)

Red Wine	750 ml
Orange liqueur	45 ml
Red apple	2
Green apple	2
White grapes	20
Peach	2
Fresh lime water/ soda sweet	120 ml

Method

In a jug or pitcher, pour the red wine and orange liqueur. Finely chop all fresh fruits and add into the jug of wine. Add the fresh lime water/ soda sweet. Chill for 45 minutes before serving.

Preparation time ~ Best prepared overnight, or 1 hour | Rating ~ Medium

Top Tip ~ This is the original Spanish version of Sangria. Based on the wine of your preference, you can also prepare this drink with a dessert wine or white wine.

Mojito

The Mojito was born in Cuba but there are claims that its name is derived either from the Spanish word *mojadito* that translates as 'little wet', or the Cuban seasoning with lime, *mojo*. Originally, aguardiente ~ a pungent predecessor of rum ~ was mixed with mint and lime. This concoction was named El Draque in honour of Sir Francis Drake. The drink subsequently evolved and a light version of rum was used to prepare the Mojito. The drink was a favourite of author Ernest Hemingway who popularised it in the La Bodeguita, a bar in Havana. There are many versions of the Mojito ~ those that involve muddling and those that use lemon chunks or those that vary the type of sugar used. Most bars have their own style but the freshness and fragrance of the mint is key. It is served tall and is best with white powdered sugar or sugar syrup. Any ice works with this drink as long as there is lots of it. A mix of crushed and cube ice works wonders.

Ingredients

Light rum	60 ml
Fresh lime wedges	2
Fresh mint sprigs	6-10
Castor sugar	1 tsp
Soda	To top

Method

Muddle mint sprigs and castor sugar in a tall glass until flavours are released. Fill the glass with ice (preferably cracked ice/ cubes work as well). Add the rum and squeeze the lemon wedge and add to the drink. Top with soda. Garnish with a mint sprig and any citrus fruit and serve.

Preparation time ~ 5 minutes | Rating ~ Difficult

Negroni

Ingredients

Gin	20 ml
Campari	20 ml
Sweet vermouth	20 ml

Method

Fill an old fashioned (rocks) glass with ice and pour the ingredients. Garnish with an orange peel, stir and serve with soda on the side.

Preparation time ~ 2 minutes | Rating ~ Easy

Matured Negroni is a recent variation of this drink, which calls for an oak cask to mature the finished cocktail for a few days or weeks. This makes the otherwise harsh drink easy on the palate.

Dry Martini

Ingredients

Gin	55 ml
Dry vermouth	5 ml

Method

Fill a mixing glass completely with ice. Wash the ice cubes. Pour the gin and vermouth and stir until mixed well. Strain the drink into a pre-chilled cocktail (Martini) glass. Wash one fresh olive and add to the drink. Press a lemon rind against the glass rim, drop and serve.

Preparation time ~ 3 minutes | Rating ~ Medium

The vodka version is also as popular and more in demand, where the vodka replaces the gin to make a vodka Martini. This drink is stirred and not shaken. To make the perfect classic Martini, the right questions have to be asked—if the drink is to be extra dry (almost no vermouth) or wet (more vermouth) or bruised (shaken). A well-made classic Martini is transparent and clear and washing the ice helps to achieve this. Stronger than most cocktails, the smoothness of a Martini depends on how chilled the drink is. More ice in a Martini ensures lesser dilution of the drink. Fruit Martinis could be shaken if fresh fruit or pulp is used to extract flavours. Delicate and flowery Martinis are best stirred with lots of ice. Always double strain (use a tea strainer along with a hawthorn) a Martini for best results.

Frozen Lemon Margarita

Ingredients

Tequila silver	45 ml
Orange liqueur	15 ml
Fresh lime juice	15 ml
Salt	A pinch

Method

In a blender, pour the Tequila, orange liqueur and fresh lime juice. Add two standard scoops of crushed ice. Add a pinch of salt and blend until slushy. Pour into a goblet, garnish with a lime wedge and serve. (Salt rim around the glass is optional.)

Preparation time ~ 5 minutes | Rating ~ Medium

In India, the Margarita is popularly served frozen with fruit flavours. The most common fruit flavours are strawberry, peach, plum and mango. Here is another variation of this drink using fresh fruit pulp or puree:

Ingredients

Tequila	50 ml
Orange liqueur	10 ml
Fresh lime juice	15 ml
Fresh fruit pulp or puree	To taste
Salt	A pinch

Method

Blend all ingredients along with ice until slushy. Pour in a large Margarita glass and serve.

Sazerac Inspired by India

Ingredients

Aniseed infused premium Indian whisky	60 ml
Orange bitters	3 dashes
Rose syrup	5 ml

Method

Chill an old fashioned (rocks) glass by filling with ice and allowing it to sit until the drink is mixed. In a separate mixing glass, add the aniseed infused whisky, orange bitters and rose syrup. Fill with ice and stir until mixed well. Discard the ice from the old fashioned glass. Strain the mix into the old fashioned glass. Stick an orange peel (traditionally lemon) on the side of the glass and serve.

Preparation time ~ Best prepared overnight, else 2 hours | Rating ~ Medium

The original Sazerac can be made thus:

Ingredients

Rye whisky	60 ml
Peychaud's bitters	3-4 dashes
Sugar cube	1
Lemon peel	

Method

In an old fashioned glass, drop three to four dashes of Peychaud's bitters and a sugar cube and muddle. Allow the bitters to dissolve by adding half a shot of rye whisky and stir. Fill with ice and pour the rest of the whisky. Stir once again to ensure proper balance. Press the lemon peel over the drink to release flavours and drop into the drink and serve. Herb liqueur and cognac also offer good traditional variations to this recipe.

El Presidente Gold

Ingredients

Aged rum	45 ml
Orange Curacao	10 ml
Grenadine syrup	5 ml
Dry vermouth	5 ml

Method

Fill a cocktail shaker with ice and add the above ingredients. Shake well and strain into a chilled cocktail glass. Garnish with an orange peel.

Preparation time ~ 3 minutes | Rating ~ Medium

Corpse Reviver

Ingredients

Cognac (fine brandy)	50 ml
Sweet vermouth	10 ml
Fresh red apple	Half

Method

Cut the apples in chunks into a mixing glass. Muddle to release the juice. Add the brandy and sweet vermouth and fill with ice. Shake well and double strain into a chilled cocktail glass. Garnish with slices of apple and serve.

The traditional version of the drink is shaken and was served as the 'hairs of the dog' ~ a name given to cocktails consumed after a heavy night but it is now almost dead in the cocktail scene. This is a variation of the original where apple brandy is replaced by fresh apple juice and shaken rather than stirred.

Preparation time ~ 5 minutes | Rating ~ Difficult

The Daiquiri

Ingredients

Light rum	45 ml
Orange liqueur	15 ml
Fresh lime juice	15 ml

Method

In a cocktail shaker filled with ice, add the above ingredients and shake well. Strain into a cocktail (Martini) glass. Garnish with a cherry and serve.

Preparation time ~ 3 minutes | Rating ~ Easy

The Daiquiri can be prepared in large volumes using a variety of fruits and is served frozen. Some of the most popular fruit daiquiris are strawberry and mango. Pineapple and litchi too make it to the cocktail list in most bars. A great drink for the tropics, it is a summer cocktail in India and is best known here. Another version of the drink uses fruit pulp or puree. Blend the fruit pulp along with fresh lime juice, sugar syrup and light rum (one could use vodka as well) and then add a generous amount of crushed or cube ice. Add a pinch of salt and blend until slushy. Pour into a brandy snifter or goblet, garnish with an appropriate fruit and serve.

Mango Bellini

Mango ~ the king of Indian fruits, is used to give a twist to the classic recipe for Bellini that will surely help to beat the summer sun.

Ingredients

Champagne or Sparkling wine	160 ml
Mango puree	45 ml

Method

In a chilled champagne flute, pour the champagne or sparkling wine. Add the mango puree and serve.

Preparation time ~ 3 minutes | Rating ~ Easy

One of Italy's favourite cocktails, the original version contains Italian sparkling wine (preferably Prosecco) and peach puree. The drink was invented in the 1930s and named after Venetian artist, Giovanni Bellini. A combination of equal parts of peach puree and peach liqueur topped with sparkling wine entices the Asian palate to this classic afternoon cocktail.

Cosmopolitan

Ingredients

Vodka	45 ml
Cointreau	15 ml
Fresh lime juice	10 ml
Cranberry juice	30 ml

Method

In a cocktail shaker, add the above ingredients with ice and shake well. Strain into a chilled Martini glass. Garnish with an orange/ lemon peel and serve.

Preparation time ~ 3 minutes | Rating ~ Medium

Whisky Sour

The most popular of sours, this classic is always prepared with a Bourbon base. The first of the sours always had egg white, fresh lime juice and sugar syrup but the present day sours can go without the egg white ~ it is a mystery though as to how egg white is substituted. Several bars in India use blended Scotch ~ this makes the drink a Scotch Sour rather than a Whisky Sour. The finest sours are prepared using hard ice, shaken for long and served straight up.

Ingredients

American whiskey	60 ml
Egg white	1
Fresh lime juice	15 ml
Sugar syrup	15 ml

Method

In a cocktail shaker, pour all the ingredients. Shake without ice (dry shake). Add ice to the shaker and shake hard. Strain into a whisky tumbler. Garnish with a lemon peel and serve.

Preparation time ~ 5 minutes | Rating ~ Difficult

Gin and Tonic

Ingredients

Gin	45 ml
Fresh lime wedge	1
Tonic	To top

Method

In a tall glass filled with ice, pour the gin and top with tonic. Squeeze the lime wedge and drop and serve.

Preparation time ~ 2 minutes | Rating ~ Easy

Most bars in India serve G&T with a slice of lime. We advise you to insist on the lime being squeezed and dropped into the drink as this imparts flavour from the juice and aroma and freshness from the lemon peel.

Navy Grog

Ingredients

Gold rum	45 ml
Orange liqueur	15 ml
Fresh lime juice	15 ml
Sweet lime juice	60 ml
Orgeat/almond syrup	10 ml

Method

In a cocktail shaker filled with ice, add the above ingredients and shake well. Pour into a tumbler along with the ice. Squeeze a wedge of sweet lime, drop into the drink and serve.

Preparation time ~ 5 minutes | Rating ~ Difficult

Piña Colada

Ingredients

Light rum	60 ml
Coconut milk	30 ml
Sugar syrup	15 ml
Pineapple juice	120 ml

Method

In a blender with ice, pour the above ingredients and blend to break the ice. Pour into a goblet with ice. Garnish with a pineapple slice and serve.

Preparation time ~ 3 minutes | Rating ~ Medium

Income Tax

Ingredients

Gin	45 ml
Sweet vermouth	5 ml
Dry vermouth	5 ml
Orange juice	15 ml
Angostura bitters	1 ~ 2 dashes

Method

In a cocktail shaker filled with ice, add the above ingredients. Shake well and strain into a chilled cocktail glass. Drop an orange peel into the drink and serve.

Preparation time ~ 3 minutes | Rating ~ Easy

Salty Dog

Ingredients

Vodka	60 ml
Sweet lime juice	120 ml

Method

Take a tall glass and rim the glass with salt and sugar. Fill the glass with ice and pour the sweet lime juice. Pour the vodka and allow it to float. Garnish with a sweet lime slice and serve.

Preparation time ~ 3 minutes | Rating ~ Medium

Innovations *or Dreams*

Innovations are like signatures ~ personal and special. Few can duplicate them. They emerge from a bartender's understanding of alcohol, his knowledge, skills and creativity. Innovations do not happen every day ~ they evolve from experimentation, achieving the right balance and finding the cocktail agreeable to the consumer's palate. These new age cocktails have no parameters or limits, they can be inspired from classics but often, experiences and exposure to food, ice creams and sorbets, department stores, spice and meat markets contribute to the birth of an innovation. Knowing your clientele helps ~ Indians like their cocktails spicy and sweet while Europeans prefer them dry—but experience, travel and exposure have gone a long way in producing flavours that were virtually unknown.

Paan Supari Martini

Ingredients

Vodka	50 ml
Sugar coated supari	12
Fresh lime wedge	1
Apple juice	30 ml
Betel leaf	1

Method

In a mixing glass, drop the paan-supari masala, betel leaf and apple juice. Muddle until flavours are released. Squeeze the fresh lime wedge and add the vodka. Fill with ice and shake well. Double strain into a chilled Martini glass. Garnish with betel leaf and serve.

Preparation time ~ 4 minutes | Rating ~ Medium

Orange Caipiroschka

Ingredients (serves 5)

Vodka	300 ml
Orange chunks	40 pieces
White sugar granules	5 tsp
Fresh lime juice	50 ml
Sugar syrup	50 ml

Method

In a flat-base glass pitcher, add the orange chunks and sugar granules and muddle until flavours are released. Add the fresh lime juice and sugar syrup and fill with crushed ice. Pour the vodka and mix well. Garnish with an orange peel and serve.

Preparation time ~ 5 minutes | Rating ~ Easy

Caipirinha ~ This national drink of Brazil is made with Cacacha (Brazilian light rum agricole) and fresh lime. The drink travelled across the globe in the Eighties and Nineties not as the original Capirinha but as Caipiroschka with vodka. The recipe of the original drink follows the same rule but requires just fresh lime chunks and sugar, muddled and filled with either crushed or cube ice. Top with Cacacha and mix well. The application is again the same as with the Caipiroschka and is a popular cocktail in the Indian subcontinent. What requires care is muddling the lime and sugar, as a hard muddle will make the drink bitter.

Cucumber Tall

Ingredients

Vodka	60 ml
Fresh lime wedge	1
Fresh cucumber	1
Fresh lime water/ soda sweet	To top

Method

In a tall glass filled with ice, pour the vodka, squeeze the juice of the lime wedge and top with fresh lime water/soda sweet. Cut a fresh slice of cucumber and drop it into the drink. Mix gently and serve.

Preparation time ~ 2 minutes | Rating ~ Easy

Masala Maar Ke

Ingredients

Light rum	45 ml
Cointreau	15 ml
Fresh lime wedge	4
Green chilli	1
Rock salt/black salt	2 pinches
Black whole pepper	6
Cinnamon syrup	10 ml

Method

In an old fashioned glass, drop whole black pepper and break with a muddler. Add fresh lime wedge, rock salt and muddle until flavours are released. Add remaining ingredients except green chilli and fill with crushed ice. Slit the chilli and drop into the drink along with a fresh cinnamon stick. Mix gently and serve.

Preparation time ~ 5 minutes | Rating ~ Medium

Summer Citrus

Ingredients

Gin	60 ml
Kafir lime wedges	6
Fresh lime juice	10 ml
Sugar syrup	10 ml
Soda	to top

Method

In a tall glass, squeeze the kafir lime wedges and drop. Add the rest of the ingredients except soda and fill with crushed ice. Top with soda and serve.

Preparation time ~ 4 minutes | Rating ~ Easy

Smokey First Flush

Ingredients

Islay Single Malt scotch	60 ml
Orange peel	1
Second flush Darjeeling tea (cold)	120 ml

Method

In a tall glass filled with ice, pour the Islay Single Malt, top with second flush tea. Take the orange peel and release the oils over the drink. Press the orange peel against the rim of the glass to bring the aroma and drop into the drink and serve.

Preparation time ~ 2 minutes | Rating ~ Easy

Twisted Sour

Ingredients

Light Rum	30ml
Dark Rum	30ml
Orange bitters	3 dash
Freshly squeezed lime juice	15 ml
Sugar syrup	15ml
Fresh orange wedge	1
Egg white (optional)	1

Method

Break the egg and separate the egg white (optional). In a cocktail shaker, pour the light and dark rum, bitters, egg white, fresh lime juice and sugar syrup. Squeeze the orange wedge and add to the shaker and fill with cube ice. Shake well and double strain into a stem glass, preferably a champagne flute. Garnish with orange rind and serve.

Preparation time ~ 4 minutes | Rating ~ Medium

Fresh Plumtini

Ingredients

Citrus vodka	45 ml
Orange liqueur	15 ml
Fresh plum	3
Fresh lime wedge	2

Method

Cut each of the plum into wedges and deseed. In a mixing glass, drop the fresh plum wedges and squeeze the fresh lime. Hard muddle to release juice. Add the citrus vodka, orange liqueur and fill with cube ice. Double strain into a Martini glass. Garnish with a plum wedge and serve.

Preparation time ~ 4 minutes | Rating ~ Medium

Bourbon Mist

Ingredients

Bourbon whiskey	60 ml
Fresh orange peel	1
Soda	60 ml

Method

In an old fashioned (rocks) glass, pour 60 ml Bourbon whiskey. Fill with crushed ice. Top with soda. Release the essential oils from the orange peel above the ice, drop the peel and serve.

Preparation time ~ 2 minutes | Rating ~ Easy

Black Grape Caipiroschka

Ingredients

Vodka	60 ml
Fresh black grapes	12
Fresh lime juice	10 ml
Sugar syrup	10 ml

Method

Muddle the fresh black grapes in an old fashioned (rocks) glass to release the flavour. Add the rest of the ingredients and fill with crushed ice. Mix well. Use a few half grapes as garnish and serve.

Preparation time ~ 4 minutes | Rating ~ Medium

Apple Cinnamon Tall

Ingredients

Light rum	60 ml
Fresh lime wedge	2
Cinnamon syrup	15 ml
Apple juice	90 ml
Red apple slices	3
Cinnamon sticks	3

Method

In a tall glass, squeeze the lime wedge and drop, add cinnamon syrup, light rum and mix well. Fill with ice cubes and top with apple juice. Add fresh apple slices and cinnamon sticks as garnish, stir and serve.

Preparation time ~ 5 minutes | Rating ~ Medium

Cognac & Chai

Ingredients

Cognac VS	60 ml
Fresh lime wedge	1
Ginger juice	5 ml
Sugar syrup	5 ml
Darjeeling tea	120 ml

Method

In a glass filled with ice, squeeze the lime wedge and drop, add the cognac, ginger juice, sugar syrup and top with Darjeeling tea and serve.

Preparation time ~ 3 minutes | Rating ~ Easy

Ananda

Ingredients

Gin	60 ml
Fresh coriander	3 sprigs
Fresh basil leaves (tulsi)	5
Fresh cucumber	2 slices
Sparkling water	90 ml

Method

Gently muddle basil in a tumbler for flavours to release. Fill with ice and add the gin, press and drop the coriander sprigs and top with sparkling water. Add slices of freshly cut cucumber to the drink and serve.

Preparation time ~ 3 minutes | Rating ~ Easy

Southern Somras

This cocktail uses traditional Indian spices and is named after the drink of the Indo-Aryans ~ Somras ~ the recipe for which is now lost.

Ingredients

Dark rum	50 ml
Orange liqueur	10 ml
Curry leaves	8
Jaggery	5 gm
Sweet lime juice	60 ml
Fresh lime wedge	2

Method

In a cocktail shaker, add the jaggery and sweet lime juice and muddle to mix and infuse the two. Add the rest of the ingredients and fill with ice. Shake well and pour along with ice into a stem goblet and serve.

Preparation time ~ 4 minutes | Rating ~ Medium

Spiced Guava

Ingredients (serves 5)

Chilli infused vodka	240 ml
Guava nectar	500ml
Fresh lime wedge	10
Tabasco	12 dashes
Black salt	3 pinch

Method

Fill half a pitcher with ice. Add the tabasco and chilli vodka. Squeeze the fresh lime wedge to release the juice. Top with guava nectar and add the salt. Mix well with a bar spoon. Garnish with a few slices of fresh guava and serve.

Preparation time ~ 4 minutes | Rating ~ Easy

Frozen Breakfast Daiquiri

Ingredients (serves 5)

Light rum	240 ml
Orange marmalade	250 ml
Fresh lime juice	90 ml

Method

In a blender, add the above ingredients. Blend along with enough crushed ice to fill a 1 litre pitcher until slushy. Pour into a glass pitcher. Garnish with fresh oranges and serve.

Preparation time ~ 4 minutes | Rating ~ Medium

Desi Bloody Mary

Ingredients

Vodka	240 ml
Green chilli paste	5 ml
Green coriander paste	10 ml
Black (rock) salt	½ tsp
Chaat masala	1 tsp
Fresh lime juice	15 ml
Honey	5 ml
Fresh tomato juice	500 ml

Method

In a glass pitcher, add the green chilli paste, coriander paste, rock salt, chaat masala, fresh lime juice and vodka and mix well. Fill with ice and top with fresh tomato juice and stir to mix well. Garnish with slit fresh green chillies and serve.

Preparation time ~ 5 minutes | Rating ~ Medium

Bartenders have struggled to get the classic Bloody Mary right even though the recipe is standard. It is probably the popularity of the drink and the known facts that has led to the consumer becoming smarter in fixing a Bloody Mary. We recommend that consumers innovate with this cocktail but keep the following recipe in mind:

Vodka ~ 60 ml • Tabasco ~ 6 dashes (Indians love it hot and spicy) • Worcestershire sauce ~ 5 ml • Fresh lime juice ~ 10 ml • Salt ~ a pinch • Fresh ground pepper ~ a pinch

Method

Pour all ingredients, in no particular sequence, into an old fashioned/ Collins glass filled with ice. Stir well. Serve with a lemon wedge on the side.

Mumbai Slurp

Ingredients

Cashewnut Feni (triple distilled)	45 ml
Cointreau	15 ml
Kala Khatta concentrate	30 ml
Sweet lime juice	30 ml

Method

In an old fashioned (rocks) glass, add the Kala Khatta concentrate, Feni, Cointreau and sweet lime juice and mix well. Fill the glass with crushed ice. Garnish with a sweet lime slice and serve.

Preparation time ~ 4 minutes | Rating ~ Medium

Adrak Panje

Ingredients

Vanilla vodka	50 ml
Thandai	10 ml
Ginger juliennes	8
Pineapple juice	45 ml
Fresh lime wedge	2

Method

In an old fashioned glass, muddle the ginger juliennes and lime wedge to release flavours. Add the remaining ingredients and fill with crushed ice. Mix well, garnish with a slice of fresh ginger and serve.

Preparation time ~ 4 minutes | Rating ~ Medium

Devil's Advocate

Ingredients

Green chilli infused vodka	50 ml
Fresh mint sprigs	5
Dry vermouth	5 ml

Method

Fill a Martini glass with ice. In a mixing glass, gently muddle the mint sprigs. Add the rest of the ingredients and stir. Empty the Martini glass of the ice and double strain the drink. Garnish with fresh mint sprigs and serve.

Preparation time ~ 3 minutes | Rating ~ Easy

Panchamrita

Ingredients

Black pepper infused vodka	50 ml
Orange liqueur	10 ml
Yogurt	60 ml
Sugar powder	½ tsp
Fresh orange peel	2

Method

In a blender with ice, add the above ingredients except orange peel and blend well. Pour into a stem goblet. Release the oils from the orange peel and press against the rim. Drop into the drink and serve.

Preparation time ~ 4 minutes | Rating ~ Medium

Green Appletini

Ingredients

Vodka	55 ml
Fresh green apple	½
Green apple liqueur	10 ml
Fresh lime wedge	1

Method

Cut the fresh green apple into small chunks. Drop into a mixing glass, add the green apple liqueur and squeeze the lime juice from the wedge. Muddle to release flavours and fill with ice. Add the vodka and shake well. Double strain into a chilled Martini glass. Garnish with fresh green apple slices and serve.

Preparation time ~ 3 minutes | Rating ~ Easy

A similar cocktail is the Sour Apple Martini. This cocktail requires vodka, apple pucker (sour apple liqueur), Cointreau and fresh lime juice. Give the ingredients a short shake and strain into a chilled cocktail glass. With the right balance, this Martini scores over other fruit Martinis.

Guava Blush

Ingredients

Resin infused light Rum	55 ml
White mint liqueur/ mint syrup	5 ml
Guava nectar	90 ml
Rose water	5 ml

Method

Add the ingredients to a cocktail shaker filled with ice. Shake well to break the ice. Pour into a tall red wine glass with or without ice. Garnish with fresh guava slices and mint sprigs and serve.

Preparation time ~ 3 minutes | Rating ~ Medium

Usque Berri Up

Ingredients

Blended whisky	60 ml
Red berry puree	20 ml
Fresh lime juice	10 ml

Method

In a whisky tumbler, pour the whisky, red berry puree and fresh lime juice and mix well. Fill with crushed ice and serve.

Preparation time ~ 3 minutes | Rating ~ Easy

O' Soma

Soma represents many things ~ it is a state of intoxication that is produced from drinking Somras. The Vedas refer to Soma as sacred and godlike ~ the drink, the plant from which it is derived and the god ~ are all the same entity.

Ingredients

Bourbon whiskey	60 ml
Jaggery	5 gm
Fresh lime wedge	2
Fresh sugarcane juice	30 ml
Rock salt	1 pinch

Method

In a mixing glass, muddle the jaggery with 30 ml whiskey until it completely dissolves. Add the remaining 30 ml whiskey, sugarcane juice, a pinch of rock salt and squeeze the lime wedge. Fill with ice and shake well. Pour the drink into a tumbler along with the ice. Garnish with two slender sticks of fresh sugarcane and jaggery.

Preparation time ~ 4 minutes | Rating ~ Medium

Sea Breeze Sparkle

Ingredients

Vodka	30 ml
Cranberry juice (chilled)	60 ml
Sparkling wine	90 ml

Method

In a chilled champagne flute, pour the vodka, add the cranberry juice and top with sparkling wine. Add a cherry/ black grape as garnish and serve.

Preparation time ~ 2 minutes | Rating ~ Easy

The original Sea Breeze is prepared with vodka, fresh lime juice and cranberry juice. This recipe can sometimes be varied with grapefruit juice instead of fresh lime juice but most spiritualists prefer the latter. A simple tall drink built over ice.

Fresh Pomegranate Martini

Ingredients

Vodka	50 ml
Fresh pomegranate seeds	2 tbsp
Fresh lime wedge	2
Sugar syrup	5 ml
Cherries	3

Method

Fill a Martini glass with ice and water and set aside to chill. In a mixing glass, muddle the pomegranate seeds and lime wedges until juice and flavours are released. Add vodka and sugar syrup, fill with ice and shake well. Empty the Martini glass and double strain the drink into it. Garnish with cherries and serve.

Preparation time ~ 5 minutes | Rating ~ Medium

Cold Coffee Cocktail

Ingredients

Kahlua	60 ml
Milk	120 ml

Method

In a blender with ice, add the two ingredients and short blend to break the ice and mix the ingredients. Pour into a tall glass. Sprinkle some coffee powder and serve.

Preparation time ~ 3 minutes | Rating ~ Easy

Black Russian ~ This drink is dedicated to Russia because of the base spirit used ~ vodka. The cocktail appeared in Belgium in 1949 and shot to fame in American bars mistakenly as a Russian export. The drink is made over a generous quantity of hard cubed ice in an old fashioned glass in the ratio of three parts of vodka with one part of coffee liqueur. Kahlua is the only coffee liqueur that suits the flavour of a Black Russian.

Gold Stinger

Ingredients

Cognac	50 ml
White mint liqueur	10 ml
Angostura bitters	5 dashes

Method

Pour all ingredients into a cocktail shaker and shake with lots of ice. Strain into a coupé glass. Garnish with a mint leaf and serve.

Preparation time ~ 3 minutes | Rating ~ Easy

Mixes and Syrups

Flavour is of foremost importance when you want to mix a drink. For this, you need to know the alcohol base ~ if you want to keep it silent or use its character to enhance the flavour and finish of the cocktail. Of course, the imagination and conceptualisation of a drink determines how it will finally look and taste. Often, the taste you wish to achieve may not be available in your kitchen or departmental store. You can make your own mixes or syrups by infusing a spirit with fruits, herbs and spices, or even prepare your own bitters and vermouth. Most signature drinks in famous cocktail bars have mixes prepared by bartenders. Their use in cocktails depends on the bartender's imagination. We give you a few simple mixes that are easy to make and can be stored over a period of time. Give it a shot and diversify your skills beyond cocktails!

DESI TIKI MIX

Ingredients

Cloves	20
Cinnamon sticks	5
Almonds	30
Sugar	500 gm
Water	2 litres

Method

In a saucepan, add one litre of water and almonds and bring to the boil. Remove the almonds when soft and blend with 250 ml of water to make a thick paste. Return this paste to the saucepan along with balance litre of water and the rest of the ingredients. Cover and reduce on slow heat. When reduced to half, strain into another container. Cool and store in a clean bottle.

PAAN SUPARI SYRUP

Ingredients

Sweet paan supari	500 gm
100 per cent apple juice	1 litre
White mint syrup	60 ml

Method

In a glass jar, pour the above ingredients and infuse for twenty-four hours. Strain the mix and store in a clean glass bottle.

ORANGE CINNAMON SYRUP

Ingredients

Cinnamon stick	100 gm
Fresh oranges	8
Water	1 litre
Sugar	500 gm

Method

Peel the oranges. In a saucepan, add the water, sugar, cinnamon sticks and fresh orange peel, cover and reduce to half with slow application of heat. Finely strain the liquid into a fresh jar and cool. Store in a clean bottle.

SWEET, SALT & SPICE MIX

Ingredients

Green chillies	6
Powdered rock salt	50 gm
Sugar	500 gm
Water	1 litre

Method

Slit the fresh green chillies and deseed. In a saucepan, add the above ingredients and the chillies and reduce the concentrate to half over slow heat. Finely strain and cool. Store in a clean glass bottle.

MY STYLE GROG MIX

Ingredients

Almonds	30
Cardamom green	10
Sugar	500 gm
Water	1 litre

Method

In a saucepan, boil the almonds until soft and then blend into a paste. Add the remaining ingredients along with the almonds into the saucepan and slow heat to reduce the mix to half. Finely strain and cool. Store in a clean glass bottle.

SWEET & SOUR TAMARIND INFUSION

Ingredients

Fresh tamarind	500 gm
Jaggery	250 gm
White mint syrup	100 ml
Apple juice	1 litre

Method

In a jar, add the above ingredients and infuse for twenty-four hours. Finely strain the liquid into a clean bottle and store.

Glossary

Adrak ~ Ginger
Alcoholic Beverage ~ This term is used for all fermented, brewed and distilled beverages that contain at least 0.5-1 per cent alcohol.
Aperitif ~ Derived from the Latin verb 'to open', aperitif refers to all alcoholic drinks that are consumed before a meal e.g. aromatised wines, bitters, sherry, port, Madiera, and Marsala.
Aromatised Wines ~ These are fortified wines to which a number of herbal flavours have been added e.g. Dubonnet and Lillet.
Bitters ~ Highly alcoholic drinks distilled from various herbal ingredients and combined with liquor e.g. Angostura and Peychauds.
Blended Whisky ~ Blend of malt and grain whiskies e.g. Johnny Walker, Chivas, Ballantines and Dewars.
Bourbon ~ This type of whisky is made with at least 51 per cent corn, matured over at least two years in new oak barrels. Everything about Bourbon is natural ~ colouring and flavouring is not permitted.
Chaser ~ When you guzzle something immediately after drinking an alcoholic beverage ~ soda and beer.
Chai ~ Tea.
Cocktail ~ A mixture of two or more beverages with an alcohol base.
Condiment ~ Ingredients used in small amounts to season a mixed drink, e.g. tabasco, bitters and grenadine.
Dash ~ Is equivalent to 1/16th of a teaspoon.
Desi ~ Local/ Indian.
Double strain ~ Using a fine strainer (such as a tea strainer) in addition to the cocktail strainer (Hawthorn) to bring more clarity in a straight up drink.
Dry ~ Anything that is not sweet is referred to as dry in an alcoholic beverage, e.g. dry Martini, dry Manhattan or dry wines.
Elaichi ~ Cardamom.
Flag ~ Pieces of small fruit like grape, cherry, olive skewered on a cocktail sword or toothpick to garnish a drink.
Fortified Wines ~ When brandy is added to wines to sweeten as dessert wines.
Frappe ~ Any liqueur or digestive served over crushed ice.
Frozen ~ A drink that is blended with lots of ice and served slushy.
Garnish ~ A drink decoration used to enhance the look of the cocktail. A garnish is always edible e.g. strawberry in a Strawberry Daiquiri.
Gulabi ~ Rose.
Highball/ tall drink ~ A term to define a tall drink served in a highball glass, e.g. Gin & Tonic, Whisky & Soda.
IMFL(Indian Made Foreign Liquor) ~ This is a term used to categorise alcoholic beverages that are diluted and bottled in India, e.g. Teachers, Black Dog, Vat 69 and Haig.
Islay Single Malt ~ Single Malt Scotch whisky from the Islay region of Scotland, usually the most pungent of all malts.
Lowball/ short drink ~ any drink that is served in a short glass with ice.
Masala ~ Indian term for spices and seasonings, e.g. coriander seeds, cardamom, cumin, cinnamon and peppercorn.
Mirchi ~ Chilli.
Mist ~ Any spirit that is served on a bed of crushed ice, e.g. Scotch Mist, Vodka Mist.
Mixer ~ Any alcoholic or non-alcoholic beverage that is mixed in a cocktail to bind the ingredients together.
Neat ~ Out of the bottle and into the glass.
On the rocks ~ Any alcohol served with lots of ice in a rocks glass.
Paan ~ Betel leaf.
Perfect ~ Equal parts of dry and sweet vermouth poured to make a perfect Manhattan or a perfect Rob Roy or a perfect Martini.
Proof ~ A term that denotes the alcohol content by volume in a spirit.
Second Flush tea ~ Tea from Darjeeling that is harvested in June and produces an amber, full-bodied, muscatel flavoured brew.
Shot ~ Short mixed drink served as a single shot to be swallowed in a single gulp.
Single Malt Scotch ~ Whiskies from Scotland that are made from malted barley and come from a single distillery, e.g. Glenfiddich, Glenlivet, Lagavulin and Glenkinchie.
Slammer ~ A shot with a carbonated mix that is slammed before gulping.
Sparkling wine ~ Wines with carbonation resulting from a second fermentation inside the bottle.
Spirit ~ Fermented and distilled beverage.
Splash ~ More than a dash but less than a 30 ml measure.
Straight ~ A spirit served without any mixture or condiment with slight dilution from ice.
Strain ~ To hold the ice behind after shaking or stirring a drink.
Supari ~ Betel nut.
Syrup/ cordial ~ Sweetened liquid that could be flavoured, added to balance a cocktail.
Thandai ~ A cold drink served during the occasion of Holi in India, this is a concoction of finely chopped almonds, fennel seeds, rose petals, cardamom, saffron, milk and sugar.
Toast ~ Raising a glass (usually containing alcohol) in celebration.
Tulsi ~ Basil.
Twist ~ A citrus peel to provide a hint of flavours to a light drink, e.g. Vodka Tonic with a twist.
Zest ~ Using the skin of a citrus fruit to impart flavours to a drink.

Acknowledgments

We would like to thank Ramesh Takulia, General Manager, Learning & Development, Indian Hotels Co; Arshad Khan and Hemant Pathak of the Blue Bar, Taj Palace Hotel; Rohit Agarwal of Lite Bite Foods; the management at the Asia Seven Restaurant and Bar, Qutub Hotel, New Delhi for providing us with the location to shoot our classics and innovations. Sumedh Prasad, the photographer, made each one of the cocktails look like a dream and was extremely flexible with the shoot schedule. We are also grateful to Shariq Khan, Rahul Singh and Praveen Kumar ~ the team at Cocktails & Dreams; Honey Dargan, Iona Kapur and Rozelle Mero for helping with the shoot, behind the scene and on camera; Ajay Singh for designing the layout; to Maneet Singh Sarla, Mamta Nainy and Anisha Chettri of Wisdom Tree for editing our work. Finally, this book is a tribute to our families who continue to unfailingly support us in many different ways.

Notes of a Dreamer

Notes of a Dreamer